EYEWITNESS
HORSE

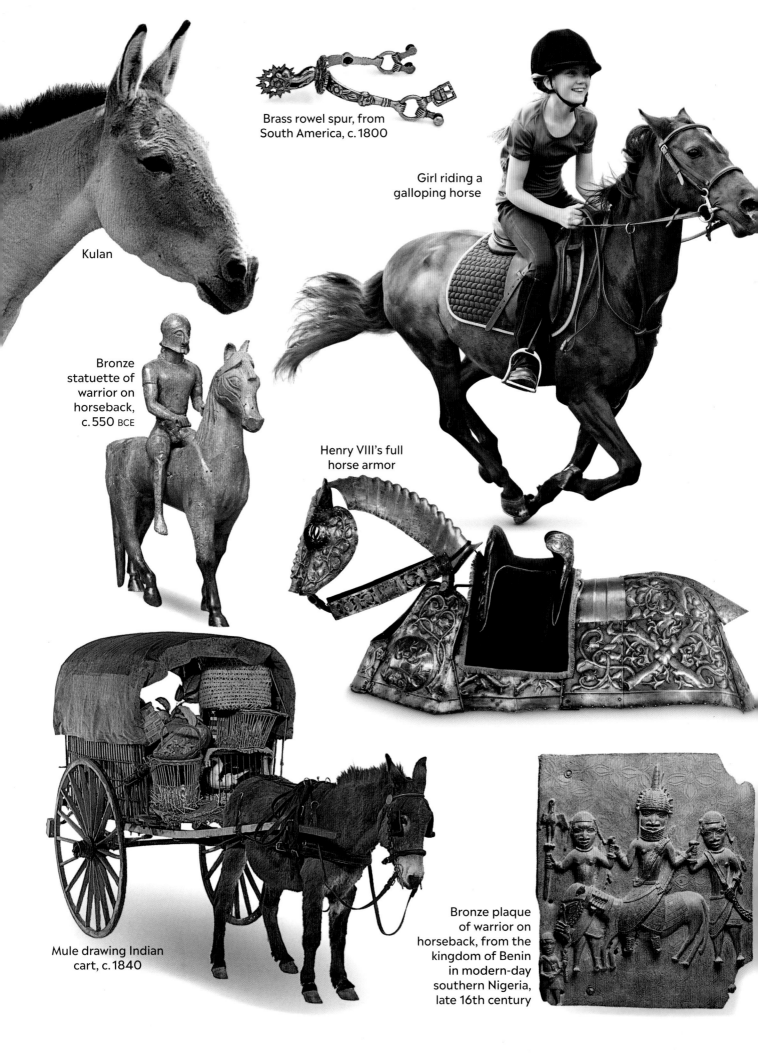

Kulan

Brass rowel spur, from South America, c. 1800

Girl riding a galloping horse

Bronze statuette of warrior on horseback, c. 550 BCE

Henry VIII's full horse armor

Mule drawing Indian cart, c. 1840

Bronze plaque of warrior on horseback, from the kingdom of Benin in modern-day southern Nigeria, late 16th century

Foot and two side toes of *Anchitherium* fossil

EYEWITNESS
HORSE

Written by
Juliet Clutton-Brock

Old shoe and nails removed from horse's hoof

Mountain zebra

Shoeing a Shire horse

Woman and girl, wearing Spanish riding costumes on dapple gray Andalusian

DK

Irish donkey pulling
cart, c. 1850

DK | Penguin
Random
House

REVISED EDITION

DK DELHI
Senior Editor Janashree Singha
Senior Art Editor Vikas Chauhan
Project Editor Abhijit Dutta
Assistant Art Editor Prateek Maurya
Senior Picture Researcher Sumedha Chopra
Managing Editor Soma B. Chowdhury
Managing Art Editor Govind Mittal
DTP Designers Deepak Mittal, Nityanand Kumar
Production Editor Pawan Kumar
Jacket Designers Juhi Sheth, Rhea Menon
Senior Jackets Coordinator Priyanka Sharma Saddi

DK LONDON
Senior Editor Carron Brown
US Editor Amber Williams
Project Art Editor Kit Lane
Managing Editor Francesca Baines
Managing Art Editor Philip Letsu
Production Controller Jack Matts
Jackets Design Development Manager Sophia MTT
Publisher Andrew Macintyre
Associate Publishing Director Liz Wheeler
Art Director Karen Self
Publishing Director Jonathan Metcalf

Consultant Dr. Debbie Nash

FIRST EDITION
Project Editor Marion Dent
Art Editor Jutta Kaiser-Atcherley
Senior Editor Helen Parker
Senior Art Editor Julia Harris
Production Louise Barratt
Picture Research Diana Morris
Special Photography Jerry Young, Karl Shone

Archer on horseback,
c. fifth century BCE

This Eyewitness ® Guide has been conceived by
Dorling Kindersley Limited and Editions Gallimard

This American Edition, 2024
First American Edition, 1992
Published in the United States by DK Publishing,
a Division of Penguin Random House LLC
1745 Broadway, 20th Floor, New York, NY 10019

Copyright © 1992, 2003, 2008, 2016, 2024
Dorling Kindersley Limited

24 25 26 27 28   10 9 8 7 6 5 4 3 2 1
001–341749–Aug/2024

A catalog record for this book is available
from the Library of Congress.

ISBN: 978-0-5938-4240-9 (paperback)
978-0-5938-4241-6 (hardcover)

Printed and bound in China

www.dk.com

French-style
barouche, c. 1880

Pair of grays with English
phaeton, c. 1840

Drum horse
and rider

Two wild
Przewalski's horses

Horse with
Western-
style bridle
and saddle

Contents

Pair of Dutch
Gelderlanders pulling
covered wagon

The horse family

Horses, asses, and zebras belong to one family of mammals named the "Equidae." They are called "odd-toed" animals because they have only one toe on each foot, whereas cows and deer have two toes and are called "even-toed." The Equidae are classified in the order Perissodactyla, alongside rhinoceroses and tapirs. All members of the horse family (equids) feed on grasses and sedges, prefer to live in groups called "harems," and use speed to escape predators. Domestic horses vary in size but they all belong to one species—*Equus caballus*. The various parts of a horse are called the "points" of the horse.

Rocking horse
Wooden rocking horses with legs on springs, or rockers, have been traditional toys for hundreds of years.

There are around
400 breeds
of horses in the world.

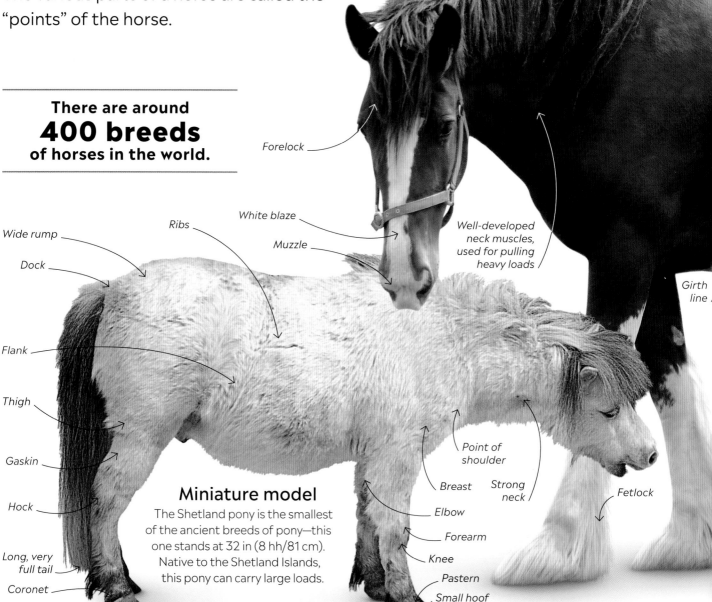

Mane

Withers

Forelock

White blaze

Ribs

Muzzle

Well-developed neck muscles, used for pulling heavy loads

Girth line

Wide rump

Dock

Flank

Thigh

Gaskin

Hock

Long, very full tail

Coronet

Miniature model
The Shetland pony is the smallest of the ancient breeds of pony—this one stands at 32 in (8 hh/81 cm). Native to the Shetland Islands, this pony can carry large loads.

Point of shoulder

Breast

Strong neck

Elbow

Forearm

Knee

Pastern

Small hoof

Fetlock

Asses and zebras

Other than the horse, the other members of the Equidae family are the Asian wild asses, the African wild asses, and the zebras.

Large ears with dark tips

No forelock

Heavy head

Dark muzzle

Short, erect mane

Pale underbelly

Kulan – a type of Asian wild ass

Long, erect ears

Typical white muzzle

Poitou donkey

Pale brown shadow between black stripes

Dark muzzle

Common, or plains, zebra mother and foal

Broad back

Very powerful rump

Measuring a horse's height

The height of a horse is measured in "hands" from the ground to the base of the neck at the top of the shoulder (withers). One hand (the width of an adult's hand) is equal to 4 in (10.16 cm). A horse measuring 15.2 hh (hands high) is 62 in (157 cm) high.

Tails are cut short to prevent snagging in harness

A great horse

The Shire horse was first bred in the English Midlands for work on farms and for pulling great weights. This breed is distinguished by its huge size and by the long hair, or "feathering," around the feet.

European travelers

Many members of the horse family, from zebras to wild asses, originated in Africa. Europeans brought domesticated horses to the continent to use as transport. This wooden carving was made by Ibo people in Nigeria, West Africa.

A unicorn is a mythical horse with a lion's tail, two-toed hooves, and a spiral horn.

Feathered feet

Huge hoof

Horse evolution

It took about 55 million years for the modern horses, asses, and zebras (equids) to evolve from their earliest horse-like ancestor. Originally called *Eohippus*, it has now been renamed as *Hyracotherium*. In the woods of Europe, North America, and eastern Asia, *Hyracotherium* was a "browsing" animal, feeding on leaves and shrubs, with four hoofed toes on its front feet and three on its hind feet. It evolved into a "grazing" (grass-eating) mammal with three hoofed toes, and later with a single hoof, on all feet. As grassland replaced woodland in North America, ancestral horses evolved longer limbs to escape predators and high-crowned teeth to chew tough grass. The first grazing horse *Merychippus* was replaced by *Pliohippus,* the first one-toed horse, and later gave rise to *Equus.*

Main hoof-core

Side view of left hind foot of *Hipparion*

Left side toe

Hoof of small side toe

Right side hoof

Main hoof-core

Front view of hind foot of *Anchitherium*

Nasal bone

Ear bone

Incisor tooth

Extinct equid

This skeleton is *Hippidion*, an extinct one-toed equid that evolved in Central America and spread to South America. Its descendant, *Onoluppidium*, survived until 12,000 years ago, at the end of the Ice Age.

Three-toed grazer

Hipparion (side view of skull, above) was the last three-toed equid. This grazer had high-crowned teeth, and its fossils have been found in Europe, Asia, and Africa. It was not extinct in Africa until about 5.3 million years ago.

Incisor for cutting food

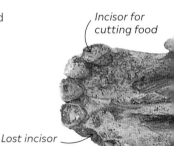

Lost incisor

EVOLUTION OF HORSES

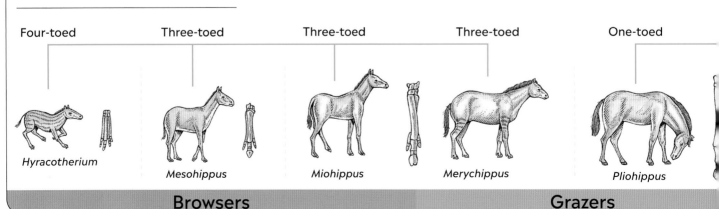

Four-toed	Three-toed	Three-toed	Three-toed	One-toed
Hyracotherium	*Mesohippus*	*Miohippus*	*Merychippus*	*Pliohippus*
Browsers			**Grazers**	

Equine sideline

The three-toed fossil horse, *Anchitherium*, spread from America through Asia and Europe about 24 million years ago. It was an equine sideline and did not evolve into the modern horse. It became extinct 5 million years ago.

Side toe

Side toe – hoof-core missing

Side hoof-core

Main hoof-core

Foot and toe bones of *Anchitherium*

Lower cheek teeth (molars and premolars)

Lower jaw of *Anchitherium*

Part of mandible (jaw bone)

Upper cheek teeth

Upper jaw of *Anchitherium*

The oldest equid

The palatal (roof of mouth) view of this *Hyracotherium* skull from 54 million years ago shows the square, six-lobed teeth from which modern horse teeth evolved.

Orbit, or eye socket

Palatal bone

Cranium for brain

Palatal view of *Hyracotherium* skull, showing roof of mouth

Parietal bone

Orbit

Nasal bone

Cheek teeth

Side view of right-half of *Hyracotherium* skull

High-crowned teeth used for chewing

Foramen magnum (hole for spinal cord)

Ear bone

Base of cranium

Palatal view of *Hipparion* skull

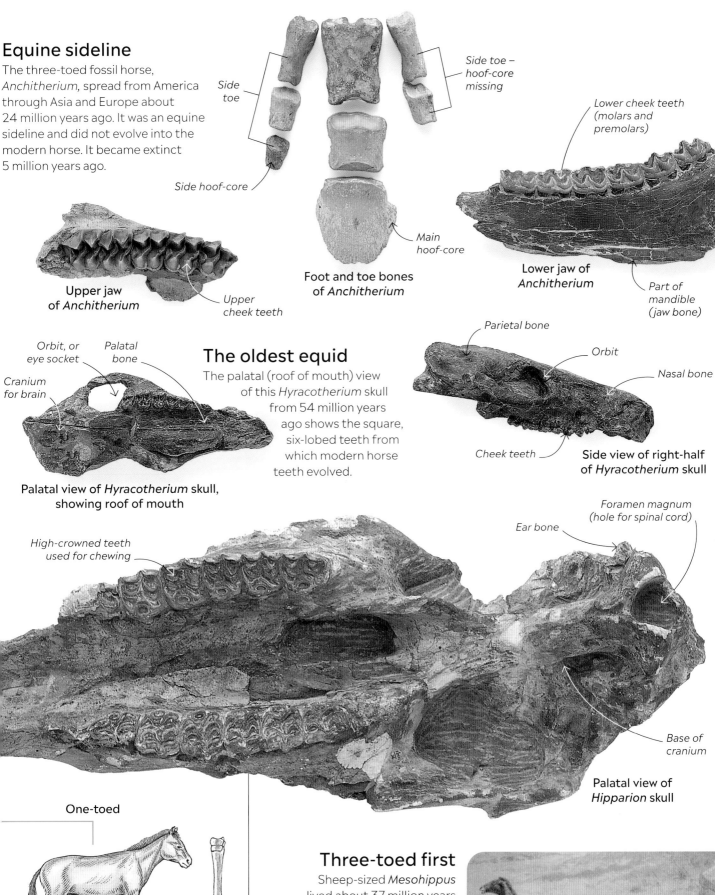

One-toed

Equus

Grazers

Three-toed first

Sheep-sized *Mesohippus* lived about 37 million years ago and was the first horse to have three toes (with the middle toe larger than the side ones).

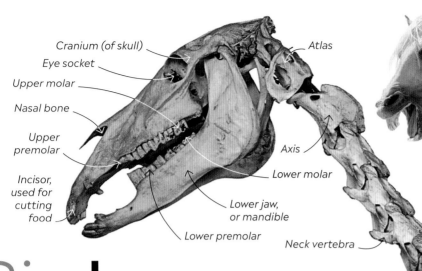

Cranium (of skull)

Eye socket

Upper molar

Nasal bone

Upper premolar

Incisor, used for cutting food

Lower premolar

Lower jaw, or mandible

Lower molar

Atlas

Axis

Neck vertebra

Long in the tooth

As a horse ages, the incisors are angled forward making it appear "long in the tooth." The incisors change from oval to round to triangular and then flattened. Experts use these signs to estimate a horse's age.

Scapula, or shoulder blade

Humerus

Big bones

The skeleton of all members of the horse family is built for speed and stamina. Wild equids use super speed and sharp vision to escape predators. The long skull contains the grinding teeth necessary to chew grass. The vertebral column keeps the back rigid, the rib cage protects the heart and lungs, and the limb bones are extended. Equids run on only a single toe. Foals are often born toothless, but the milk teeth come through the soft jaw bones. These temporary teeth are replaced by adult teeth. Generally, an adult male equid has 40 teeth—12 incisors, 4 canines, 12 premolars, and 12 molars. As horses age, their teeth gradually wear down, change shape, and become very discolored.

Skeleton of a racehorse

Radius

Knee

Metacarpal, or front cannon, bone

First phalanx, or long pastern bone

Second phalanx, or short pastern bone

Hoof

EYEWITNESS

Gillian Higgins

British horse physiotherapist and expert in anatomy, Gillian Higgins teaches people about how bones and muscles work together by painting them onto the horses's coats. She travels the world teaching "Horses Inside Out."

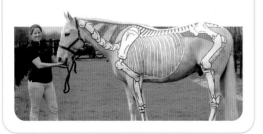

Classic skeleton

In 1766, English artist George Stubbs (1724-1806) published *The Anatomy of the Horse,* which is still used for reference more than 200 years later. He dissected horses to show bone construction.

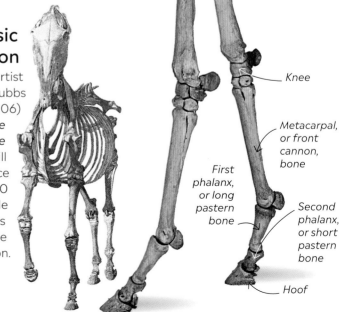

Upper jaw of newborn horse

Straight from the horse's mouth

The foal's milk teeth wear down after it is weaned and begins to graze, and are replaced by adult teeth. The adult teeth have short roots and long crowns. These wear down but then regrow, lasting their lifetime.

Adult molar starting to develop

Milk premolar

Milk canine

Milk incisor

Adult molar starting to develop

Adult molar, ready for cutting

Milk premolar

Adult premolar

Milk incisor

Upper jaw of two-year-old pony

Upper jaw of six-year-old pony

Molar, for grinding food

Premolar, for chewing food

Incisor, for cutting food

Upper jaw of aged horse

Spinal vertebra

Hip bone

Pelvic girdle

Femur

Tail vertebra

Stifle joint

Molar almost worn away

Premolar

Incisor

Rib

Mighty muscles

This anatomical drawing by George Stubbs shows the amazing muscle structure of the horse, which enables it to travel long distances, jump great heights, and haul big loads.

There are about 25 species of horse chestnut tree in North America, Europe, and Asia. In the late 1500s, the seeds were used to treat respiratory illnesses in horses, so this is how the tree got its name.

Tibia

Hock joint

Metatarsal, or hind cannon, bone

Skeleton shape

The shape of a horse's skeleton depends on its breed. A carthorse has huge bones to support the muscles needed to haul heavy weights, while a racehorse (shown above) has long, slender bones built for galloping along at high speed.

First phalanx

Second phalanx

Hoof

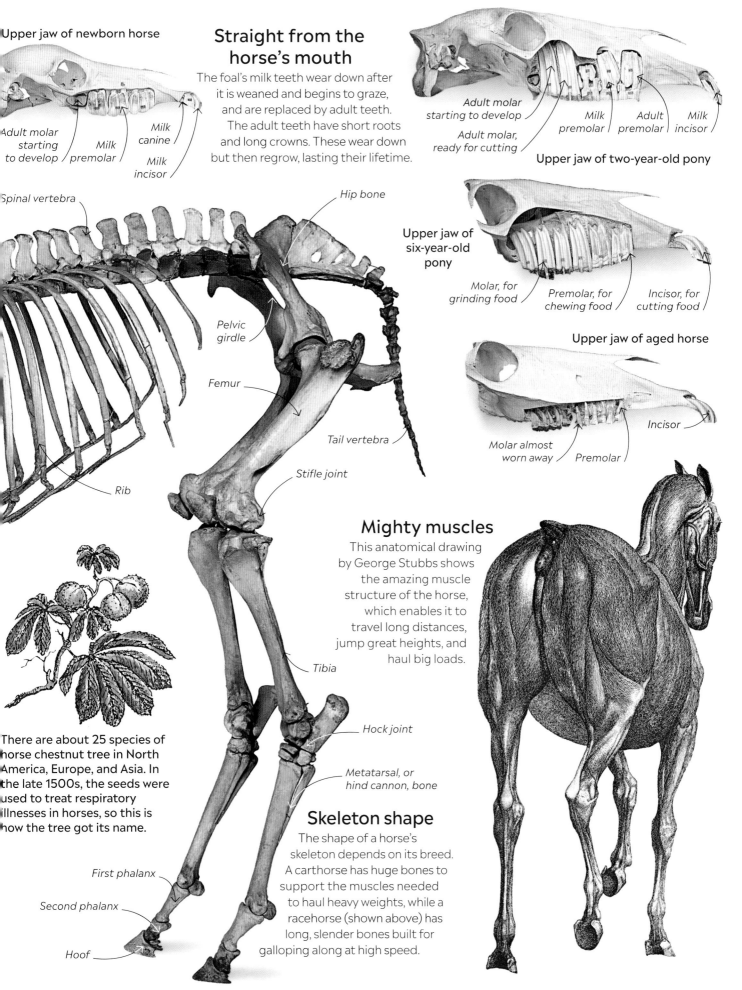

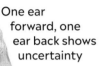

Ears pointing back show submission or fear

Ears pointing forward show interest in surroundings

One ear forward, one ear back shows uncertainty

Super senses

Horses, asses, and zebras have better senses of sight, hearing, and scent than humans. The long face of the horse not only houses the large teeth, but also the sensitive smell organs. Eyes set high in the skull on either side of the head provide all-around vision. Ears are large, and in the asses very long, so they can point toward any sound. The horse, a herd animal, shows affection to other group members, and this loyalty is easily transferred to a human owner. This strong bond means horses will follow commands. The domestic horse and donkey retain the natural instincts and behavior patterns of their wild ancestors, such as defending their territory and suckling their foals.

Two-way stretch

An equid's ears have a dual role—to pick up sounds and transmit visual signals. If a mule (shown above) puts its ears back, it is frightened or angry. If forward, it is interested in what is happening. One ear forward and one back means it is not sure what will happen next.

Rolling over

This pony is having a good roll, as part of grooming. It relaxes the muscles and helps to remove loose hair, dirt, and bugs.

A bite threat

These Assateague wild horses from two different herds are trying to show who is the more dominant, with one showing a bite threat to the other. The attacking horse's neck is thrust forward, ready to bite.

Laid-back ears
showing anger

Kick
threat

Flehmen reaction

Pulling back his lips and drawing
air in over his vomero-nasal organ
after smelling a mare's urine, this
stallion is seeing if she is ready to
mate. This is the flehmen reaction.

Kulan's kick

The laid-back ears and threatening kicks
show that these kulans are not getting
along too well.

The best of friends

Two horses will often stand
close together, head to tail,
nuzzling each other's manes and
backs, thus establishing their
relationship. These grooming
and cleaning sessions usually
last about three minutes.

Ears pointed forward
or "pricked," showing
that the horse is
on alert

Bite given to
unfamiliar horse

Protecting territory
and family

Fighting by rearing and sparring
with the front hooves is natural to
all equids. But they can also settle
differences by threats with their ears,
tails, and back hooves. Stallions fight
over territory or to protect their
mares, like these Konik stallions.

**Equids have the
largest
eyes
of all land
mammals.**

Mares and foals

A mare—or female horse, ass, or zebra—gives birth to a foal after a carrying-time (gestation period) of about 11 months. The long gestation period ensures the foal is healthy enough to keep up with the herd from birth. The herd lives on open grasslands where food can be scarce, and the young are an easy target for predators. As soon as it learns to walk, the foal tries to keep up with its mother. Under four years of age, a female foal is called a "filly" and a male foal a "colt." In the wild, fillies and colts leave their mothers' herds to form new groups as they mature.

A pregnant Palomino

The large belly on this Palomino shows she will soon give birth. All equids give birth quickly. Domestic horses are often watched in case something goes wrong.

The **foal stands** within **an hour of its birth** and begins grazing in weeks.

Watch out!

All modern day equids are descended from horses that have been domesticated for thousands of years, but this mare still has the protective instincts of her wild ancestors.

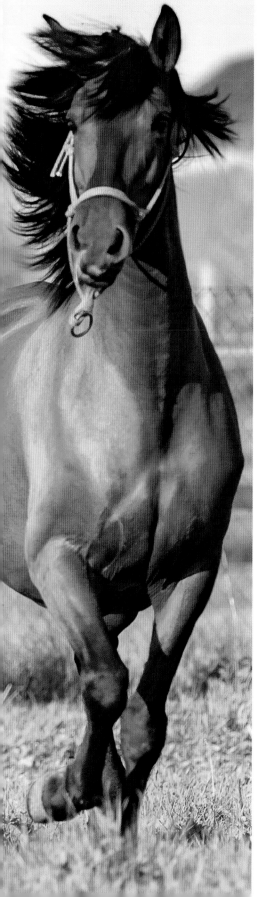

A newborn foal

This mare is resting after giving birth to her foal. The mare and foal have moved apart from each other, enabling the umbilical cord to break naturally.

After giving birth, the mare eats to gain stamina.

The mother is very protective of her foal.

First drink

As soon as it can stand, the foal finds and sucks the mother's teats. The first milk ("colostrum") helps a foal build immunity to disease.

First steps

While the mother grazes, she is still alert for danger. The foal takes its first faltering steps.

... And so to bed

Like all babies, a foal must rest, but it can stand quickly in case of danger.

Wild asses

Catch your onager
These scenes of catching wild onagers alive, c. 645 BCE, are from stone friezes in the palace of Nineveh in present-day Iraq. These now-extinct Syrian onagers may have been caught for cross-breeding with domestic donkeys or horses.

The three species of wild ass are not closely related. They include the true wild ass of Africa (*Equus africanus*), which ranged over the Sahara Desert in North Africa, and the two species of Asian wild asses—the onager (*Equus hemionus*) from Southwest Asia and northwest India, and the kiang (*Equus kiang*) from the Tibetan plateau, China. Of these, the African wild ass is the ancestor of the domestic donkey. All wild asses look similar, with a heavy head, long ears, short mane, no forelock, slender legs, and a wispy tail. They are adapted for life in the semi-deserts and mountains of Africa and Asia. Today, they risk extinction from habitat loss and hunting.

Long, wispy tail

Slender, pale-colored leg

Preservation
There were several races of African wild ass until recently. The Somali wild ass (*Equus africanus somaliensis*), the only African ass in the wild, has been taken to an Israeli wildlife park to try to save the species.

Now extinct?
The Nubian wild ass (*Equus africanus africanus*) is extremely rare, and might have become extinct already. However, more research is needed to confirm this.

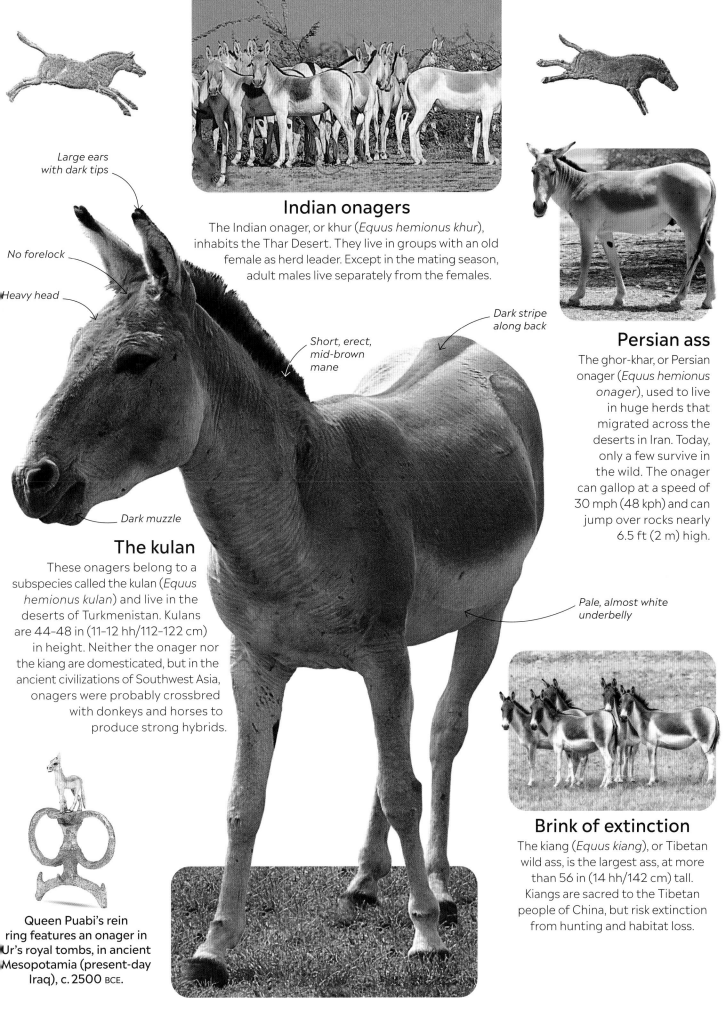

Indian onagers

The Indian onager, or khur (*Equus hemionus khur*), inhabits the Thar Desert. They live in groups with an old female as herd leader. Except in the mating season, adult males live separately from the females.

Large ears with dark tips

No forelock

Heavy head

Short, erect, mid-brown mane

Dark stripe along back

Dark muzzle

Persian ass

The ghor-khar, or Persian onager (*Equus hemionus onager*), used to live in huge herds that migrated across the deserts in Iran. Today, only a few survive in the wild. The onager can gallop at a speed of 30 mph (48 kph) and can jump over rocks nearly 6.5 ft (2 m) high.

The kulan

These onagers belong to a subspecies called the kulan (*Equus hemionus kulan*) and live in the deserts of Turkmenistan. Kulans are 44–48 in (11–12 hh/112–122 cm) in height. Neither the onager nor the kiang are domesticated, but in the ancient civilizations of Southwest Asia, onagers were probably crossbred with donkeys and horses to produce strong hybrids.

Pale, almost white underbelly

Queen Puabi's rein ring features an onager in Ur's royal tombs, in ancient Mesopotamia (present-day Iraq), c. 2500 BCE.

Brink of extinction

The kiang (*Equus kiang*), or Tibetan wild ass, is the largest ass, at more than 56 in (14 hh/142 cm) tall. Kiangs are sacred to the Tibetan people of China, but risk extinction from hunting and habitat loss.

Seeing stripes

Large, rounded ears

Today, zebras live only in Africa but their ancestors, like all horse family members, evolved in North America. There are three living species of zebra – Grevy's, common, and mountain – in different habitats with different stripe patterns. Zebras feed on coarse grass and cross wide areas to graze. They are very social, spending time on grooming and nuzzling each other. Zebras live in family groups of 100 or more. Scientists know that a zebra's stripes help keep flies away, but they don't know why flies avoid stripes in particular.

Big ears

The Grevy's large, round ears can signal to other zebras and listen out for distant sounds.

Zebroid

Zebras can interbreed with all other horse species, but their offspring are infertile. This zorse is a hybrid between a zebra and a horse.

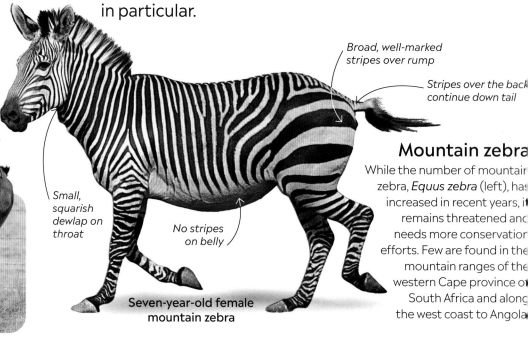

Broad, well-marked stripes over rump

Stripes over the back continue down tail

Small, squarish dewlap on throat

No stripes on belly

Seven-year-old female mountain zebra

Mountain zebra

While the number of mountain zebra, *Equus zebra* (left), has increased in recent years, it remains threatened and needs more conservation efforts. Few are found in the mountain ranges of the western Cape province of South Africa and along the west coast to Angola.

Common or plains

The common zebra, *Equus burchelli*, at 52 in (13 hh/132 cm), once ranged throughout eastern and southern Africa. It is still common and herds can be seen in most wildlife reserves.

Grevy's zebra

Grevy's zebra, *Equus grevyi*, inhabits the semi-desert areas of Kenya, Ethiopia, and Somalia. It is the largest zebra, standing about 56–60 in (14–15 hh/142–152 cm). It is considered to be a relic of more primitive horse family members.

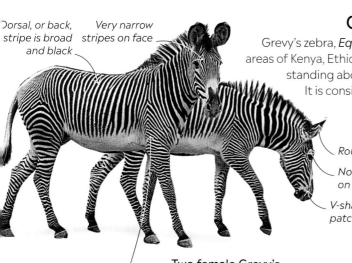

Dorsal, or back, stripe is broad and black

Very narrow stripes on face

Rounded ears

No forelock on head

V-shaped, brown patch on nose

Narrow, closely spaced black stripes on a white background

Two female Grevy's zebras, aged three to four years

Very tall, erect mane

White on either side of black dorsal stripe

Broad hooves

Stripes go down legs and end at the black coronet, next to hoof

Zedonk

Cross-breeding between a zebra and a donkey can produce finely striped brown animals, such as this zedonk from Zimbabwe.

The quagga

A fourth species of zebra, the quagga (*Equus quagga*), was found by 19th-century colonizers in southern Africa. Quaggas were hunted to extinction, but attempts are now being made to recreate the species by selectively breeding plains zebras.

👁 EYEWITNESS

Grevy's Zebra Trust

Set up in 2007, this charitable organization aims to conserve Grevy's zebra because only 3,000 remain in the wild. The trust works in Kenya to save the endangered species. It works with local communities to conserve the habitat of the species and monitor and protect them.

A herd of zebras at a watering hole in the Serengeti National Park in Tanzania

Ancient ancestors

At the end of the last Ice Age, 10,000 years ago, millions of horses, *Equus ferus*, lived wild across Europe and Asia. They roamed in herds and migrated annually. As grassland replaced forest, their numbers dropped from habitat loss and hunting until few were left. The first wild horses were tamed and domesticated in present-day Russia about 6,000 years ago, soon spreading westward. Modern domestic horses are descended from these ancestors and they are classified in one species, *Equus caballus*.

Extinct wild horse
Many 18th-century travelers to Russia saw small wild horses, called tarpan (*Equus ferus ferus*). They died out in the early 1800s. In Poland today, ponies similar to the tarpan have been bred from primitive breeds, such as the Konik.

Height range at withers 52–56 in (13–14 hh/132–142 cm)

Short mane

Short forelock

Light-colored muzzle, typical of wild horse

An ancient English pony
The Exmoor pony is an ancient breed that closely resembles the extinct tarpan, or wild pony, of eastern Europe. The ponies live in feral herds on Exmoor in England.

Sacred white horse

White horses were sacred to the Celts of western Europe. In about 500 BCE, a horse shape was scraped into the chalk hills at Uffington, Oxfordshire, in England.

A helping hand

Przewalski's mare and foal at the San Diego Zoo

The San Diego Zoo in California is playing an important role in the preservation of species, such as the Przewalski's horse and Grevy's zebra. Such efforts are significant in ensuring that these endangered species are not lost.

Przewalski's horses

Wild Przewalski's horses (*Equus ferus przewalskii*) were found in Mongolia in the 1880s, with a few bred in European zoos. They have been extinct in the wild since the 1960s, but are being reintroduced to Mongolia from herds bred in captivity.

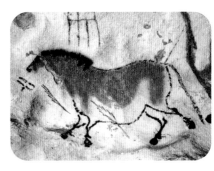

Mongolian horses

While coming from the same place as the Przewalski's horse, the Mongolian horse is a different species, dating back to the 12th century. They are kept by nomads and provide transport, milk, hair, meat, and dung for use as fuel. The annual Mongol Derby is the longest horse race in the world, recreating the route of the long-distance postal system set up in 1224.

Long, shaggy tail

Group of Przewalski's horses

Cave paintings

This wild horse (*Equus ferus*) was painted on a wall in the famous caves at Lascaux in France by hunting people toward the end of the last Ice Age, about 14,000 years ago.

Wild African ass

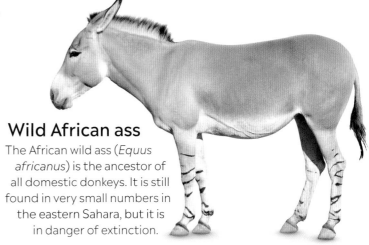

The African wild ass (*Equus africanus*) is the ancestor of all domestic donkeys. It is still found in very small numbers in the eastern Sahara, but it is in danger of extinction.

Horses in **history**

The earliest evidence for the domestication of the horse comes from Russia, around 6,000 years ago. Even 1,000 years before that, the African wild ass was being domesticated in ancient Egypt and Arabia. Horses and asses were harnessed in a pair to a chariot, which became a status symbol of kings. By the 8th century BCE, riding horses and donkeys was a popular means of travel. The ancient Greeks and Romans built special sporting arenas for chariot races.

The end of the day

This horse's head is from the Parthenon marbles (5th century BCE) in Athens, Greece. Legend goes that horses pulled the Sun's chariot to the sea each day to make the sunset, so the horse's face looks exhausted.

Royal standard

This early depiction of donkeys harnessed to a cart is on a mosaic box—the Standard of Ur—in the royal tombs of Ur in ancient Mesopotamia (present-day Iraq).

A horse called **Copenhagen** was **ridden** for **17 hours** during the Battle of **Waterloo**.

Flying through the air

In Greek mythology, the winged horse Pegasus sprang from the blood of Medusa when Zeus's son Perseus cut off her head. Athena caught Pegasus during its flight to join the gods and tamed it with a golden bridle. This engraving of Pegasus was made by the Etruscans in about 300 BCE.

Half man, half horse

The myth of the centaurs—half men and half horses—may come from sightings of the horsemen of Thessaly in ancient Greece. People were unfamiliar with men on horseback, so they thought this was a new being. This scene shows the battles between the wild centaurs and the Lapiths of northern Greece.

Ready for war

This terra-cotta model from Cyprus shows an Assyrian warrior. His horse has a breastplate and headdress.

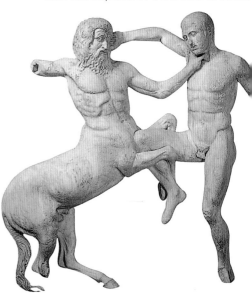

The four horses of Venice

Thought to be the work of 4th-century-BCE Greek sculptor Lysippus, these bronze horses were taken from Constantinople (now Istanbul) in 1204 CE, to the San Marco Basilica in Venice.

Hunting on horseback

This hunting scene is from a mosaic pavement (c. late 5th or 6th century BCE) discovered at Carthage, a city founded by the Phoenicians near modern-day Tunis. The mosaic was made in North Africa and shows a favorite pastime of wealthy landowners—hunting.

Decorative piece on the forehead of the horse

Surprise!

During the Trojan War of 1184 BCE, the Greeks invaded Troy by hiding soldiers inside an enormous wooden horse. The Trojans later famously wheeled the horse into the city.

A bit of a Tang

During the Tang Dynasty in China (618–907 CE), many earthenware models of horses were produced that are of great artistic value today. The cobalt-blue glaze was rare and expensive to produce because cobalt was imported in very small quantities. This figure would have been molded in several parts and then joined as a whole.

Donkey work

The domesticated ass, or donkey (*Equus asinus*), is descended from the African wild ass (*Equus africanus*), from the deserts of the Sahara and Arabia. In that harsh environment, the donkey has developed strength, stamina, and endurance to carry heavy loads long distances on little food and water. In the wild, donkey foals develop fast to keep up with the herd when it travels to find food. Female donkeys, or jennies, carry their foals for 11–14 months before birth. The donkey, like the horse, thrives in groups.

Jesus on a donkey

When Jesus was born, the donkey was the usual means of transport in Jerusalem. The "cross" on a donkey's back and the fact that Jesus rode a donkey on the first Palm Sunday, made people believe that these hairs had healing powers.

Greek harvest

In Greece, until recently, it was a common sight to see donkeys threshing grain. By walking around in a circle, the donkeys' hooves separate the seeds and husks.

Water, water

Water is the most precious resource in desert countries. This Sudanese woman is attending her donkey, loaded with water containers.

Donkey herders

In Turkmenistan, donkeys are still used to help with herding and farm work.

Poitou donkeys

In the Poitou region of France and in Spain, there has been a tradition of breeding large donkeys to mate with female horses and produce giant mules for farm work. Poitou donkeys stand 56 in (14 hh/142 cm) at the shoulder, or withers, making them the world's largest donkeys.

Donkeys of Ireland

Donkeys are the traditional pack and haulage animals of Ireland. Having been bred here for centuries, they have adapted to a climate very different from the deserts in which they evolved. Irish donkeys have thicker coats and much shorter legs than donkeys from hotter regions.

Mid-19th-century English donkey cart

Rein

Breeching straps around animal's haunches

Terret

Rein ring

Bridle

Blinker

Bit

Collar

Nose band

Trace

Wooden shaft

Girth strap

Footstand for stepping up into cart

African donkeys

These donkeys are drinking from Lake Magadi in Kenya. Out in the open, they must fend for themselves and learn to keep away from predators.

Regal white donkeys

Donkeys are popular pets on farm parks. This has led to breeding for new looks, like this white donkey. In ancient times, these white donkeys were favored by royalty.

Long ears

Long tail, with tuft at tip

Well-trimmed hooves

If the thick, soft coat of the Poitou donkey is not groomed, it hangs in long cords called "cadanettes."

Mules and hinnies

The Sumerians of Mesopotamia were the first people to interbreed horses and donkeys to produce mules (horse mother, donkey father) and hinnies (donkey mother, horse father) about 4,000 years ago. For thousands of years mules have been used as pack animals to carry huge loads, because they combine donkey stamina with horse strength. Like its parents, a mule is a herd animal that travels well in a "mule train" (a long line of mules harnessed together to pull loads). All the species in the horse family can interbreed, but the resulting offspring will be infertile.

Ancient Egyptian equids

This ancient Egyptian tomb painting from c. 1400 BCE shows a pair of horses drawing a chariot, while below two white hinnies are also pulling one. Their smaller ears show they are hinnies, not mules.

Long, ass-like ears of its father

During a hard day's travel, a working mule feeds from a nose-bag filled with oats.

Breast collar is easier to fit than larger collars

Crate of ducks

Indian travel

Mule carts have been used in Asia for 3,000 years. Early carts were attached by a wooden pole to a pair of mules, or horses. The idea of putting an animal between two wooden shafts was invented only 2,000 years ago. Above, the mule has a bridle with a bit and is driven with reins. The family's goods are piled into the cart.

Large wheel makes it easier for the animal to pull this load

14-year-old mule, 55 in (13.3 hh/140 cm), drawing Indian cart (c. 1840)

A powerful mule

Mules traveled faster than oxen and were more sure-footed than horses, so 19th-century colonizers preferred these animals for hauling huge loads over very muddy roads on their long trek west across North America.

Heavy head with long ears

Large body

Neat front legs

Strong hind legs

Long tail, like a horse

Short ears

No forelock, like a donkey

Tourist class

People often enjoy a leisurely drive in a carriage, like this mule-drawn carriage in New Orleans. Mules and horses in the tourism industry have to work hard. Many places have laws to ensure that they are not overworked, are fed well, and have regular checkups.

Cross-breeding

When a donkey is crossed with a horse, the foal has what is called "hybrid vigor"— meaning it is stronger and has more stamina than either of its parents. The most common cross-breed is a donkey stallion (or jack-ass) with a horse mare, which produces a "mule," but if a horse stallion is crossed with a female donkey (or jenny) the hybrid offspring is called a "hinny" (or jennet). Generally, a mule is a stronger animal than a hinny.

Stubborn as a hinny

This eight-year-old white hinny will not be pulled where it does not want to go. Donkeys, mules, and hinnies have a reputation for being stubborn, but this is because their behavioral patterns are misunderstood. These intelligent herd animals are nervous of going to new places alone. Once trained to follow a person, they will go anywhere.

Dark grey spots on white, short-haired coat

Long, tufted tail, used for swishing flies, or to show it is anxious

Misbehaving mule

Eight-year-old hinny

27

New shoes

Equid hooves are made of "keratin," a protein like hair or human fingernails. Hooves can be cut and shaped without hurting the animal. On flat land, hooves wear down evenly, but on stony or hard roads, these wear excessively and may split and break. On soft ground, they become overgrown and cause discomfort and mobility issues. A horse receives regular attention from a "farrier," who is trained to look after hooves and fit protective metal shoes. The hoof consists of the outer "wall," the "sole," and wedge-shaped "frog."

1 Remove old shoe
The horse stands patiently while the farrier carefully levers off the worn old shoe.

Old horseshoe and nails just removed from horse's hoof by farrier

Indian shoes
Methods of shoeing horses have been the same worldwide for centuries. In this drawing, three workers are shoeing a horse during the time of the Mughal emperors in northern India, c. 1600 CE.

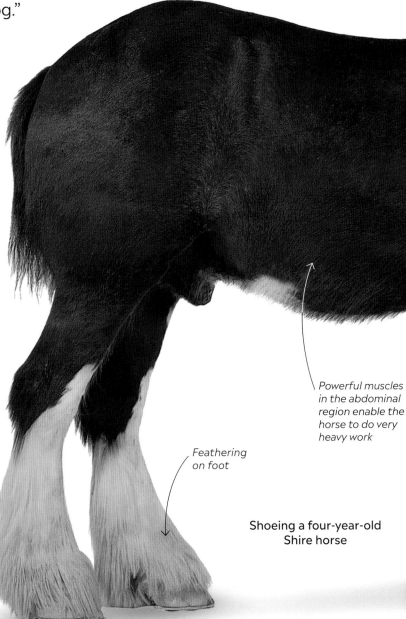

Powerful muscles in the abdominal region enable the horse to do very heavy work

Feathering on foot

Shoeing a four-year-old Shire horse

Farrier's box of essential tools for shoeing horses

"Horn," or horseshoe-shaped excess hoof growth, removed by farrier

2 Hoof clean
The excess hoof is clipped and the hoof is filed and cleaned so it is ready for the new shoe.

3 At the forge
The farrier makes a new iron shoe at the forge. Using a heavy hammer, the farrier shapes the shoe on an anvil and adds holes for the nails.

Good luck
A horseshoe is a lucky talisman. It is held with the open part at the top, so that good luck does not drop out. Horseshoe pitching—a game of luck—is played in the US and Canada.

Height at withers 70 in (17.2 hh/178 cm)

4 Steaming
At the stables, the shoe is reheated, pressed onto the hoof to check the fit, and then allowed to cool down. The hoof gives off a smell of burning hair and much smoke, but this does not hurt the horse.

Chestnut

6 Finished foot
The foot rim is filed before the farrier hammers it flat. Nails must be flush with the shoe, and the hoof and the outer shoe edge should match.

Filing hoof and nail ends flat

Balancing on one front foot

5 Nailing on the shoe
The farrier hammers special iron nails through pre-drilled holes in the shoe. Nail ends showing through the hoof are wrung off and turned back.

When "hippo" meant "horse"
Before iron horseshoes, the Romans tied a shoe of wicker or metal to the hoof with leather, called a "hipposandal" (*hippo* in Greek means "horse").

Hipposandal, French, 1st–3rd century CE

Bits and **pieces**

Back view of a person riding sidesaddle

The earliest domestic equids were ridden bareback, guided by a rope tied around the lower jaw. The first bits, or bridles' mouthpieces with fastenings at each end to which reins are attached, were made of hide, bone, or wood. In about 1500 BCE, bronze and then iron replaced them. Until late Roman times, people rode bareback. There were no saddles or stirrups (loops suspended from a saddle to support the rider's foot) in Europe until the 8th century CE. Despite this, riders from Eurasia and the Americas could shoot arrows from a galloping horse. One powerful ancient nomadic horse people were the Scythians of Central Asia in the 4th century BCE.

Spurred on

Horses in 13th-century Europe had a hard time, for they were bridled with bits and goaded by armored knights wearing cruel spurs (U-shaped devices attached to the rider's boot heel).

Rowel spur (length 9 in/23 cm), made of iron and brass, western European, early 1500s

Rowel

Screw would have clamped stirrup to outside of shoe

Metal part of stirrup would have fitted inside heel of shoe

Tiny rowel spur (length 1.5 in/4 cm), made of iron and fitting directly onto shoe, European, late 1600s

Buckle for attaching stirrup to boot

Metal part of spur for "pricking" horse

Prick spur (total length 11 in/29 cm), made of iron, Moorish, early 1800s

Putting your foot in it

The Chinese probably invented metal foot stirrups in the 5th century CE. Stirrups spread westward to Europe. They influenced the battlefield, allowing riders to wield their weapons without falling off.

Iron stirrup, Bulgar, 800–900 CE

Decorated boot stirrup, made of iron, Spanish, 1600s

Brass fretwork

Box stirrup, made of painted wood and brass fretwork, French or Italian, late 1700s

Dragon decoration

Brass stirrup, decorated with two dragons, Chinese, 1800s

Joint   Rein ring

Jointed snaffle bit, Irish, 100 BCE–100 CE

Build a better bit

Several types of bit control domesticated horses. The simple "snaffle" bit changed into a jointed mouthpiece in Assyria, c. 900 BCE. A "curb" bit is unjointed with a chain under the horse's chin, which applies pressure with reins. A "pelham" bit combines two bits of a double bridle in one.

Joint   Rein ring

Cheekpiece

Jointed snaffle bit with cheekpiece, Bulgar, 800–900 CE

Detail from the Bayeux tapestry from France, c. 1080

Defeat in battle

In the Battle of Hastings, 1066 CE, William the Conqueror's troops beat the English. One reason for victory was their use of stirrups, while the English dismounted to fight on foot.

Double rollers in horse's mouth

Curb chain   Rein ring

Brass boss

Curb bit made of steel and brass, European, 1500s

Sidesaddle

Headpiece

Brow band   Throatlash

Height at withers 68 in (17 hh/173 cm)

Bit   Rein

Sidesaddle

This bay horse is being ridden sidesaddle. Women today usually only ride like this in the show ring or out hunting. In former times, from the early 1300s onward, the sidesaddle was the main way a rider, wearing long, heavy skirts, could be mounted on a horse.

Exploring by horse

Viking chessman

This 12th-century knight on horseback carving is one of the famous chessmen from Scotland's Isle of Lewis.

Without the horse and the ass, human history would have been quite different. People could not have explored and conquered. Invading forces needed fast transport and efficient movement of goods, weapons, and food to overcome the defenses of settled communities. Horse riding was a common form of transport from 1000 BCE, but it was in the 11th century CE that horses were shod, and a saddle and stirrups used. From this time, the horse became important in war, sports, and travel.

Genghis Khan

Genghis Khan (1162–1227 CE), the Mongolian conqueror, ruled an empire of nomadic horsemen that stretched across Asia into Europe.

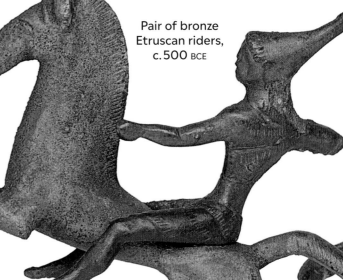

Pair of bronze Etruscan riders, c. 500 BCE

Holy Roman Emperor

Charlemagne, or Charles the Great (742–814 CE), was the most famous ruler of the Middle Ages. In 796 CE, he led 15,000 horsemen against the Avars in Hungary, and later became Emperor of the Holy Roman Empire.

Statue of Charlemagne, the Holy Roman Emperor

Archers of the ancient world

These two Etruscan bronzes from Italy show how Scythian archers shot arrows from galloping horses. The archer shooting backward exemplifies the "Parthian shot," a technique used by nomadic horsemen on the steppes of central Asia.

In the saddle

This 18th-century wooden saddle is probably similar to the one used by Genghis Khan 600 years before.

Fretwork

Pommel

Cantle

18th-century saddle from Tibet, China

Alexander the Great

Bucephalus, a black stallion born c. 331 BCE, is probably the most famous horse to have ever lived. He belonged to Alexander the Great (356–323 BCE), and together they conquered much of the known world – from Greece to Egypt and Afghanistan.

Stone frieze of Alexander the Great on his horse, Bucephalus (left), on a sarcophagus in Syria

Horses have almost 360-degree field of vision.

Patron saint

St. George is the patron saint of cavalry (soldiers who fight on horseback). He is also the patron saint of England, Portugal, Georgia, and more.

Archer showing "Parthian shot"

Golden wonder

This exquisite gold model of a four-horse chariot, c. 5th century BCE, is from the Achaemenid Empire of Persia (present-day Iran).

Part of treasure found near the River Oxus in central Asia

Tassel on bridle

Curb ring

Curb chain

Gold embroidery on felt, stitched onto leather backing

Reins

Early 19th-century North African bridle with curb bit

To the Americas

Indigenous people have been living in the Americas for 15,000 years—long before European colonizers arrived in 1492. The Europeans brought with them fast horses and mules. A few horses escaped into the wild, and a century later, they had spread over the grasslands. Indigenous groups bartered with each other for their own stock and learned to ride.

Gauchos
The gauchos of the South American pampas work on huge ranches. They spend their lives in the saddle.

Man Who Carries the Sword
This 19th-century painting, created by an artist of the Oglala Lakota people, shows an Indigenous warrior on horseback. The warrior is wearing a headdress decorated with feathers. There are feathers on his shield as well, showing that he was a person of renown. The horse has a silver bridle.

Central wooden shaft, or "tongue," to which harness is attached

Horses return
In the early 1500s, Spanish conquistadors brought horses to the Americas, where they had been extinct for 10,000 years. The Indigenous peoples tamed escaped horses that had become feral.

Blaze

Martingale

Stocking

Shod hoof prevents excessive wear

Westward, ho!

Indigenous people were already living on the Pacific coast when European missionaries, trappers, and traders reached the Pacific. In 1843 a band of 1,000 colonizers left Missouri on the 2,000-mile (3,300-km) trek westward along the Oregon Trail. It took many months to reach their destination.

Beasts of burden

Before there were railways across North America, teams of mules would haul heavy wagons along muddy roads and across treacherous rivers.

Mobile home

Early European colonizers traveled across North America in a covered wagon, or "prairie schooner." They had to be mostly self-sufficient, knowing how to shoe a horse, mend a wheel, and bake bread.

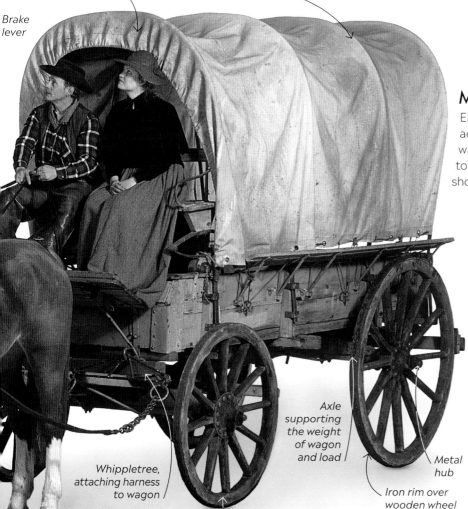

Waterproof heavy-duty canvas top

Canvas held up by iron hoop underneath

Brake lever

Whippletree, attaching harness to wagon

Pair of Gelderlanders
(66 in/16.2 hh/168 cm)

Front wheel, 4 ft (123 cm) across, is smaller for sharp turns

Axle supporting the weight of wagon and load

Metal hub

Iron rim over wooden wheel

👁 EYEWITNESS

Paul Revere's Ride

Revere and his horse became legends when American poet Henry Wadsworth Longfellow wrote "Paul Revere's Ride." On the night of April 18, 1775, Paul Revere rode from Boston to warn the residents of Concord, Massachusetts, about approaching British troops.

Running wild

There are no longer any truly wild horses, but there are many herds of horses and ponies described as "feral." These are descended from domesticated stock, but they live and breed in the wild. The last truly wild horses, the Przewalski's horses, survived in Mongolia until the 1960s. Now, they are found only in zoos and wildlife parks. In the Americas, horses spread rapidly over the grasslands after the first Europeans brought horses and donkeys in the 15th century. Soon large herds of these animals were living wild all over the grassland and deserts.

Fell ponies

In Britain many breeds of pony live on the moors, like the Fell pony. Although Fell ponies are owned, they can live and breed with little human control.

German Dülmen

These rare ponies live semi-wild on the Duke of Croy's estate in Westphalia in Germany. They have been cross-bred with British and Polish ponies, so they are not pure-bred. The herd dates back to the 1300s.

The brumby of Australia

There have been feral horses in Australia for 150 years, ever since they were abandoned during the gold rush. Called brumbies, these horses reproduced in big numbers over vast areas. Since the 1960s, they have been hunted to such an extent that in some locations very few remain.

Dawn in the Camargue

The beautiful white horses from the Camargue in the south of France have lived wild in the marshes of the Rhône delta for over 1,000 years. They have very wide hooves, adapted for life on wet grassland.

Symbolic horses

A wild running horse has often been used as a symbol of freedom and elegance. It has advertised many things, from banks to sports cars—such as Mustang in the US, and Ferrari, the supreme speedster.

The mustangs of America

The feral horses, or mustangs, of the US's Nevada Desert have hard lives traveling far and wide in search of grass and water.

Przewalski's horse is the last known horse subspecies that qualified as **truly wild**.

The ponies of the New Forest

Herds of ponies have lived in the New Forest woodlands of Hampshire, England, since the 11th century. For 800 years, these ponies lived wild, but in the 19th century efforts were made to improve them by bringing in stallions of other breeds. They still run wild here, but are also reared on stud farms and used as riding ponies.

Gray
This coat is black skin, with a mixture of white and black hairs, as in this Connemara pony from Ireland.

Horses of
the world

Breeders often divide horses into three types. First are "hotbloods"—the Arabs and the Thoroughbreds. These horses descended from the Arab and Barb breeds of hot countries in North Africa and Arabia. Second are "coldbloods," which are the heavy draught horses of cold, northern climates. Third are "warmbloods"—crosses between hotbloods and coldbloods. Most modern sports horses, except Thoroughbred racehorses, belong to this group. All Thoroughbreds descend from three stallions: the Byerly Turk (c. 1689), the Darley Arabian (c. 1702), and the Godolphin Arabian (c. 1731).

Dapple-gray
This coat color occurs when dark gray hairs form rings on a gray coat, as in this Orlov Trotter from Russia.

Palomino
Palomino (a color, not a breed) is a gold coat, with flaxen tail and mane, as in this Haflinger pony from Austria.

Aristocratic Arab

The Arab has an elegant head, slender limbs, and spirited nature. Arabs have been carefully bred, and records kept of their pedigrees in both North Africa and Arabia.

Chestnut
Chestnut occurs in various shades of gold—from pale gold to a rich, red gold, as in this French Trotter from Normandy, France.

Bridle

"Dished," or concave, profile is typical of Arabs

Four-year-old, pure-bred Arab, mahogany bay in color

Bay
This is a reddish coat, with black mane, tail, and "points" (ears, legs, and muzzle), as in this Cleveland Bay from England.

Coronet is white hair just above the hoof

Sock is the white hair reaching between the fetlock and the cannon bone

Brown
Brown is mixed black and brown in coat, with brown mane, as in this Nonius from Hungary.

Height at withers 59 in (14.3 hh/150 cm)

Stocking is the white hair reaching up to the knee, or hock

EYEWITNESS

Lalla Fatma N'Soumer

Fatma was born into the Kabyle family of Imazighen. Like most Imazighen, she was an expert rider. Often compared to Joan of Arc, she was one of the main leaders of the military campaigns against the French invasions of Algeria in the mid-1800s. She led several battles against the invading forces until her capture in 1857.

Rearing up

As horses are beautiful and can be trained easily, they are ridden in shows, where they can perform natural movements, but on command.

15-year-old Arab, very light gray color with tiny dapples in coat

Embroidered saddle-cloth

Barbs and Imazighen

The Barb, second only to the Arab as the first horse breed, is the traditional mount of the Imazighen of North Africa.

Height at withers 57 in (14.1 hh/145 cm)

Horse fair

Horses have been sold at horse sales for centuries, as shown in this detail of a painting by English artist, John Herring (1795–1865).

Other breeds
and colors

Every country has its own horse breeds. Breeds are defined by their size and body shape, color, and any white markings on the face and legs. Horses come in different sizes. The smallest horse, the Falabella, measures 30 in (7.2 hh/76 cm) at the withers. The largest breed, the Shire horse, stands 68 in (17 hh/173 cm) or more and weighs about a ton. A horse's color impacts its skin. Pale ones can get sunburn, mostly around the eyes and muzzle.

Height at withers 65 in (16.1 hh/165 cm)

Stars...
It is usual for horses to have white facial markings, such as a regular, or irregular, "star" shape high on the face. An example is this Danish Warmblood, a breed now regarded as Denmark's national horse.

... And stripes
A strip of white, extending from above the eyes to the nostrils, is called a "stripe," as on this Oldenburg, a breed established in Germany in the 1600s.

What the blazes!
A wide strip above the eyes and extending down the muzzle is a "blaze," as on this Gelderlander from the Netherlands. When white hair covers almost all the face, it is called a "white face."

Seven-year-old, dark gray, pure-bred Andalusian ridden by a woman in classical Spanish riding costume

Classical equitation
The Spanish Riding School, in Vienna, Austria, was founded in 1572 with Lipizzaner horses.

Horses in art

The beauty and strength of the horse has inspired sculptors and artists for thousands of years, such as this stylized work by German painter, Franz Marc (1880–1916).

The "Spanish Horse"

Known as the "Spanish Horse" for centuries, Andalusian horses were first bred by Carthusian monks at Spanish monasteries in the 1400s. Today's horses are bay or grey, but they were originally chestnut or black.

Sheepskin saddle cover on which the rider sits

Spanish-style saddle blanket

Exhibiting spectacular passage, a slow-tempo trot with exaggerated elevation of legs

Black

Horses are called black when the coat, mane, tail, and legs are completely black, as in this Friesian from the Netherlands.

Bay

This is one of the most common colors seen in domestic horses. The horse has a reddish-brown or brown coat with black mane, tail and lower legs.

Dun

This color can be a blue, mouse, or light yellow coat (with black in the legs, mane, and tail), as in this Norwegian Fjord pony. The "dorsal eel stripe" seen on the mane and back is typical of this breed.

Spotted

A spotted coat can have five varieties of pattern, usually dark spots on light hair, as seen here in this minute Falabella, first bred in Argentina.

Skewbald

Skewbald is white patches on another coat color, except black. This Pinto pony has a chestnut coat with white patches ("Ovaro").

Piebald

Piebald means large, irregular patches of white and black hairs in the coat, as in this Shetland pony.

War horses

The horse and the ass have been used in wars for 5,000 years. By riding in chariots harnessed to a pair of horses, men could travel fast and cause damage to the enemy. When armed horseriders (cavalry) arrived at the time of Alexander the Great, the horse played a big role in all wars until after World War I, when mechanized vehicles took over. As better fitting and secured saddles were introduced, longer weapons could easily be used on the battlefield.

Peytral to protect breast

Tibetan warrior

For centuries, the Tibetan cavalry used armor made of small metal plates (lamellae) laced with leather thongs. This armor, for horse and rider, was used by the nomadic warriors of central Asia. The Tibetans in China have preserved this armor.

Tibetan cavalry armor, used from the 17th to 19th centuries

 EYEWITNESS

Marengo

Marengo was the white Arab horse ridden by French leader Napoleon Bonaparte (1769–1821). Named after the Battle of Marengo in 1800, the stallion carried the French emperor in four other battles, including the Battle of Waterloo in 1815.

Ghanaian warrior

This brass model of a warrior on horseback was cast in Ghana in West Africa during the 18th century.

War Horse

Based on Michael Morpurgo's book by the same name, *War Horse* premiered at UK's Royal National Theatre in 2007. Set against the backdrop of World War I, the play revolves around the horse Joey and his friendship with a young boy Albert, showcasing the deep bond between people and animals.

Three men formed the head, body, and hind legs of Joey.

Australian artillery

The Waler breed (named after New South Wales in Australia where horses were first imported 200 years ago) was considered to be the finest cavalry horse used during World War I. Walers were strong and hardy, able to carry heavy loads, and had good stamina.

During WWI, the USA shipped around 1,000 horses daily to the British army.

Into battle

The Charge of the Light Brigade—resulting in huge casualties of both horses and men—was the most disastrous battle of the Crimean War (1853–1856), fought between Russia on one side and Britain, Turkey (Türkiye), France, and Sardinia on the other. The Crimea is a small area of land to the north of the Black Sea.

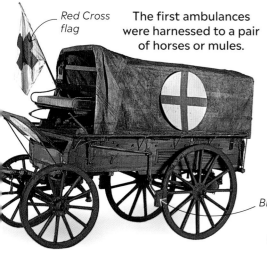

Red Cross flag

The first ambulances were harnessed to a pair of horses or mules.

Brake

WWI necessities

Pack horses and mules hauled essential supplies of food, water, and arms to the Front Line.

World War I water wagon, made in England, used in France, hauled by two horses

19th-century British cavalry spur, made of nickel silver

Stirrup

The stirrup was the most important innovation in the history of the horse in war because it enabled a heavily armed rider to stay on his horse.

The age of chivalry

In the 11th century, Europe saw the rise of knights, who were feudal lords, owning land and controlling agricultural laborers or serfs. They were Christians, bound by the religious and moral code of chivalry. As well as knowing how to fight, the ideal knight was brave, courteous, and loyal to their king.

Samurai warrior
This painting depicts a 12th-century Japanese samurai warrior in battle. The honorable samurai was totally loyal to his feudal lord.

European, late-19th-century brass copy of 15th-century medieval spur with rowel, which was long to reach under the horse's armor

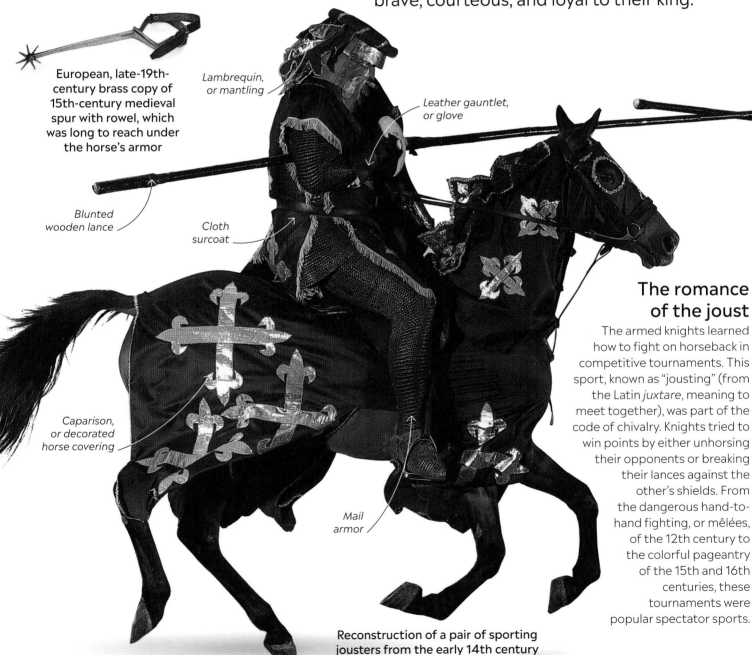

Lambrequin, or mantling

Leather gauntlet, or glove

Blunted wooden lance

Cloth surcoat

Caparison, or decorated horse covering

Mail armor

Reconstruction of a pair of sporting jousters from the early 14th century

The romance of the joust
The armed knights learned how to fight on horseback in competitive tournaments. This sport, known as "jousting" (from the Latin *juxtare*, meaning to meet together), was part of the code of chivalry. Knights tried to win points by either unhorsing their opponents or breaking their lances against the other's shields. From the dangerous hand-to-hand fighting, or mêlées, of the 12th century to the colorful pageantry of the 15th and 16th centuries, these tournaments were popular spectator sports.

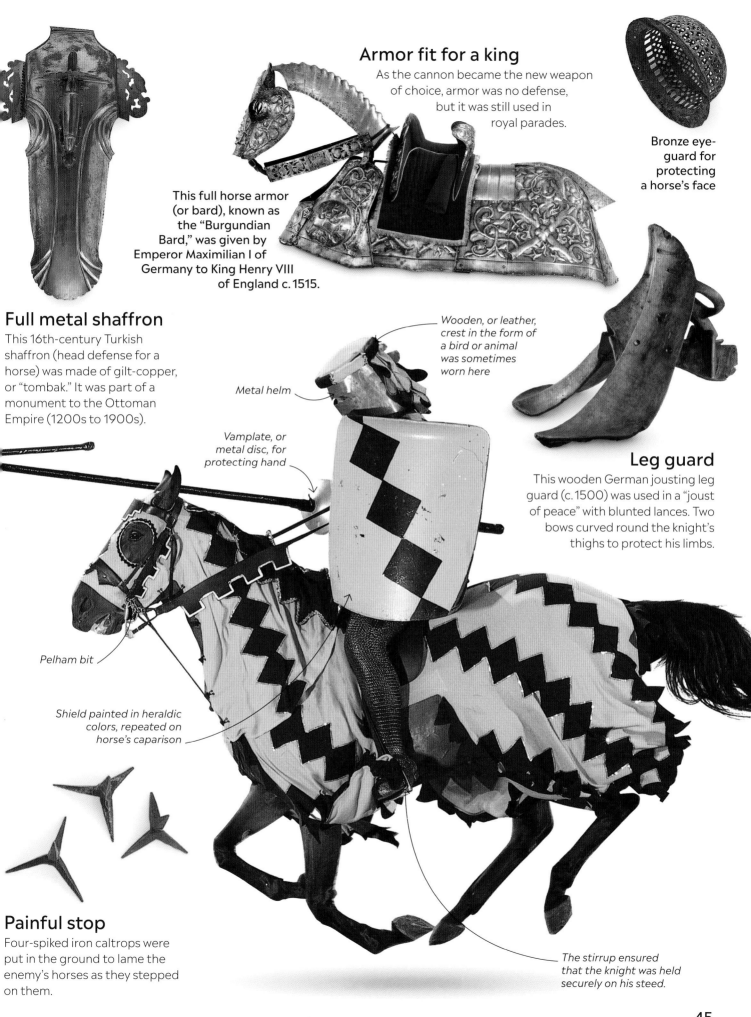

Armor fit for a king

As the cannon became the new weapon of choice, armor was no defense, but it was still used in royal parades.

Bronze eye-guard for protecting a horse's face

This full horse armor (or bard), known as the "Burgundian Bard," was given by Emperor Maximilian I of Germany to King Henry VIII of England c. 1515.

Full metal shaffron

This 16th-century Turkish shaffron (head defense for a horse) was made of gilt-copper, or "tombak." It was part of a monument to the Ottoman Empire (1200s to 1900s).

Wooden, or leather, crest in the form of a bird or animal was sometimes worn here

Metal helm

Vamplate, or metal disc, for protecting hand

Leg guard

This wooden German jousting leg guard (c. 1500) was used in a "joust of peace" with blunted lances. Two bows curved round the knight's thighs to protect his limbs.

Pelham bit

Shield painted in heraldic colors, repeated on horse's caparison

Painful stop

Four-spiked iron caltrops were put in the ground to lame the enemy's horses as they stepped on them.

The stirrup ensured that the knight was held securely on his steed.

45

Traveling by horse

Horses, asses, and mules have carried people and goods for more than 4,000 years. The first harness and carts were made of wood, bone, and leather, until 3,500 years ago when copper and bronze were used on chariots, followed by iron 1,000 years later. Metal additions to harnesses sped up travel times in southern Europe and Asia. But in rainy northern Europe, the pack horse remained the best mode of travel until roads were built by the Romans and built again in the Middle Ages (1100–1500 CE).

Fit for a queen

This is a replica of Queen Elizabeth I's carriage—the first carriage to be built for the British monarchy. Until then, royalty rode in carts. With steps folded up the side, the carriage's padded roof protected against rain.

Adorning horses

The horses of the Indigenous peoples of North America have endurance and stamina for life on the plains. The Apsáalooke value horses as community members and craft ornaments to honor them. This chief of the Apsáalooke people rides a horse that is wearing a collar decorated with traditional motifs.

> All **four hooves** leave the ground together in a **gallop**.

Highway robber and horse

Dick Turpin (1705–1739) was a legendary English highway robber who, it has been recorded, rode from London to the city of York in record time on his mount Black Bess.

Jane Dotchin

Dotchin and her dog Dinky trek on her pony Diamond from Hexham in north England to Inverness in the Scottish Highlands every year. Jane, now in her 80s, has made this 600-mile (966-km) journey since 1972. It takes around seven weeks to complete.

Beast of burden

This stone frieze shows that the ancient Assyrians bred powerful mules to carry hunting gear.

Pilgrims' progress

Pilgrim riders featured in the *Canterbury Tales* by 14th-century poet Geoffrey Chaucer.

18th-century bronze horse and rider from the kingdom of Benin (present-day southern Nigeria)

Patron saint

St. Christopher (3rd century CE) was patron saint of travelers. His feast day is July 25.

Canvas-covered barrel top

Caravans

For many centuries, Romani people have traveled around Europe in their caravans. Some Romani still use these as mobile homes, as well as a place to conduct business.

Horse-drawn vehicles

Early chariots in the ancient world had solid wooden wheels and a fixed axle that did not pivot. The invention of light, spoked wheels allowed chariots to travel faster. The four-wheeled carriage, with a swiveling axle that could turn independently, was a feature by the early Middle Ages. The poor took carts and horse buses, while the rich traveled in grand, horse-drawn carriages. Horses were fed well and shod. Wheels were greased and repaired, and carriages were kept clean and dry.

Elegant and expensive carriage harnessed to a pair of beautiful horses

Bronze model of horse and carriage, Eastern Han Dynasty, China, second century CE

Two pairs of Welsh Cobs hauling a Wells Fargo stagecoach, made in the US, late 1800s

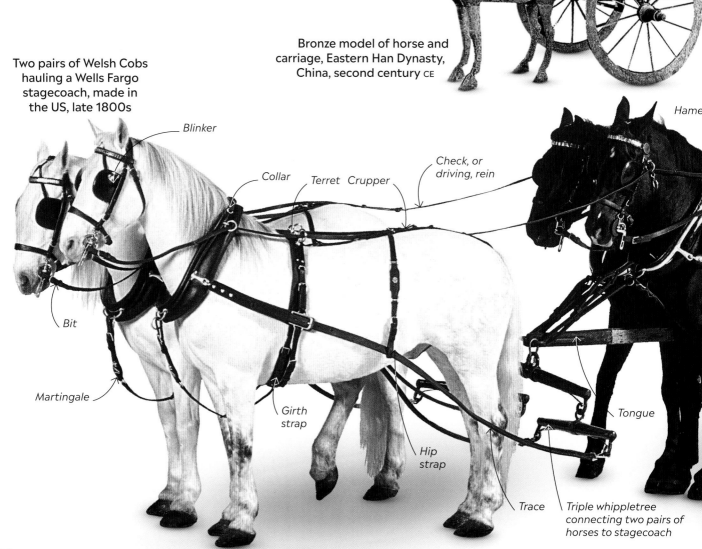

Blinker

Collar

Terret Crupper

Check, or driving, rein

Hame

Bit

Martingale

Girth strap

Hip strap

Tongue

Trace

Triple whippletree connecting two pairs of horses to stagecoach

Only one seat left on this overcrowded horse bus—two people will be disappointed

Driver's seat

Seating for two passengers

A type of Victorian carriage called a barouche, made in England from a French design, c. 1880

Way out West

Two Americans—Henry Wells (1805–1878) and William Fargo (1818–1881)—opened banking and shipping services in San Francisco in 1852, linking the Far West with the rest of the nation. The Wells Fargo stagecoaches carried passengers, money, and valuables.

"Jehu," or driver

Guard-messenger riding shotgun

Extra luggage stowed on top

Roll-up leather curtains to let in cool air, or to keep out snow and rain

Seating inside for nine passengers

Passengers' luggage stowed in rear trunk

WELLS FARGO & CO. OVERLAND STAGE

U.S. MAIL

Brake lever controlled by driver's foot

Step for passengers getting into stagecoach

Box under driver's seat containing tools, water bucket, mail pouches, and strongboxes full of valuables

Standing room for 12 passengers

Driver's seat

Hunting brake with driver's seat and space for standing room only

49

Heavy horses

In Europe and Asia, "the age of the horse" lasted from the classical times of Greece and Rome until the start of the 19th century when they were overtaken by the steam engine. Until then, the horse, mule, and donkey were the main means of transport and essential to agricultural work. They were used in forestry, harvesting, threshing on the land, and drawing water from wells. In the damp soil of northern Europe, powerful heavy horses were needed to plough and haul. Today, Europe's heavy horses are exported worldwide.

Haymaking in Ireland
The horse and the donkey are still used on small farms in Ireland. Here a wagon is being loaded with hay, which is winter food for the farm animals.

Belgian compact
Also called Brabant, this ancient breed of heavy draught horse from Belgium is pure-bred. It is still used on farms in the US.

Chestnut-colored Belgian draft horse

Deep in the forest
Heavy horses have traditionally been used to haul heavy logs from forests.

Decorated mane

Horse brass

Hame, on heavy collar

Bridle

Collar

Chain trace

Before the tractor
The invention of the rigid, padded horse collar by the Chinese, c. 500 CE, spread across Asia to Europe. This impacted agriculture, as horse-drawn plows became the tractors of their day. Today plowing with horses is slower than using a tractor, but it is better for the land. Plowing competitions take place at agricultural shows in Britain and Europe.

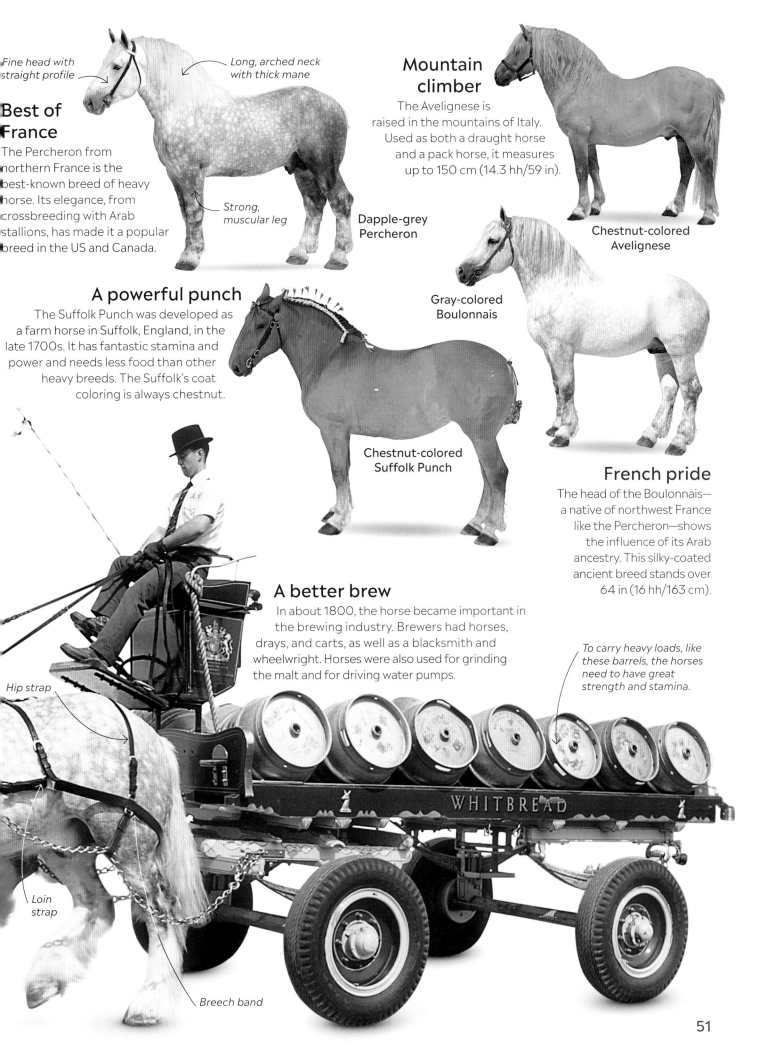

Fine head with straight profile

Long, arched neck with thick mane

Best of France

The Percheron from northern France is the best-known breed of heavy horse. Its elegance, from crossbreeding with Arab stallions, has made it a popular breed in the US and Canada.

Strong, muscular leg

Dapple-grey Percheron

Mountain climber

The Avelignese is raised in the mountains of Italy. Used as both a draught horse and a pack horse, it measures up to 150 cm (14.3 hh/59 in).

Chestnut-colored Avelignese

A powerful punch

The Suffolk Punch was developed as a farm horse in Suffolk, England, in the late 1700s. It has fantastic stamina and power and needs less food than other heavy breeds. The Suffolk's coat coloring is always chestnut.

Gray-colored Boulonnais

Chestnut-colored Suffolk Punch

French pride

The head of the Boulonnais— a native of northwest France like the Percheron—shows the influence of its Arab ancestry. This silky-coated ancient breed stands over 64 in (16 hh/163 cm).

A better brew

In about 1800, the horse became important in the brewing industry. Brewers had horses, drays, and carts, as well as a blacksmith and wheelwright. Horses were also used for grinding the malt and for driving water pumps.

To carry heavy loads, like these barrels, the horses need to have great strength and stamina.

Hip strap

Loin strap

Breech band

WHITBREAD

51

Horse **power**

Without the horse, the Industrial Revolution could never have taken place. Horse transport enabled manufactured goods to be carried to ships for export abroad and enabled people to flock to cities for industrial work. Factory horses provided power to engines and machines for grinding malt or wheat, spinning cotton, or furnace blowing. Ponies went down the mines to haul loads from the coal face and also towed coal-filled barges along canals. Today machinery has replaced horses, but the term used to measure an engine's pulling power is still "horsepower."

Cog

Horse buses
The first public horse carriages in Britain started in 1564, but roads were so bad that people could not go far.

Heavily laden coal wagon, made in England, 1920

Weighing scales

Brake

Sack of coal

Snowshoes
In heavy snow, surefooted horses are needed to haul logs out of forests, or sleds full of goods, like these horses in Lódz in central Poland.

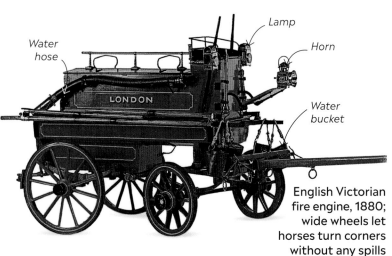

Water hose

Lamp

Horn

Water bucket

English Victorian fire engine, 1880; wide wheels let horses turn corners without any spills

Exploring the interior
Horses hauled wagons laden with supplies to Australia's interior. Today, people can travel on a horse-drawn tram in Victoria Harbor, South Australia.

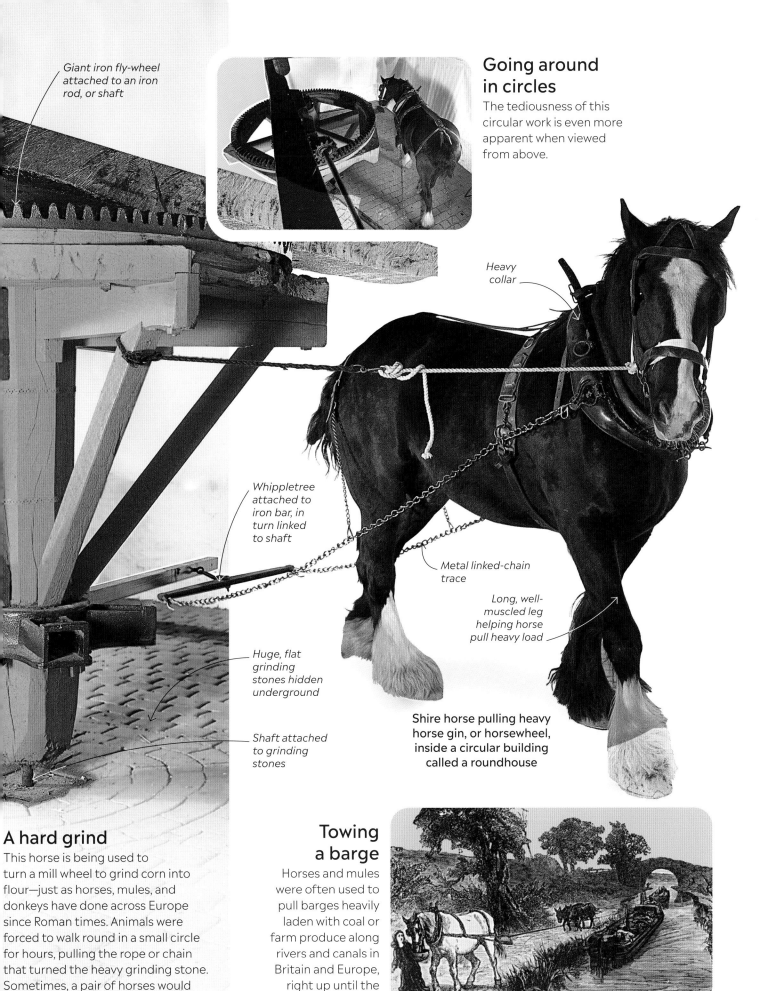

Giant iron fly-wheel attached to an iron rod, or shaft

Going around in circles

The tediousness of this circular work is even more apparent when viewed from above.

Heavy collar

Whippletree attached to iron bar, in turn linked to shaft

Metal linked-chain trace

Long, well-muscled leg helping horse pull heavy load

Huge, flat grinding stones hidden underground

Shaft attached to grinding stones

Shire horse pulling heavy horse gin, or horsewheel, inside a circular building called a roundhouse

A hard grind

This horse is being used to turn a mill wheel to grind corn into flour—just as horses, mules, and donkeys have done across Europe since Roman times. Animals were forced to walk round in a small circle for hours, pulling the rope or chain that turned the heavy grinding stone. Sometimes, a pair of horses would carry out this operation.

Towing a barge

Horses and mules were often used to pull barges heavily laden with coal or farm produce along rivers and canals in Britain and Europe, right up until the 20th century.

Light draft work

Transportation depended on the common light draft horse until the steam engine was invented in the 1820s. Such horses were powerful and fast, pulling wagons, carriages, and carts. They did not belong to a particular breed, but some, like the Cleveland Bay of Yorkshire, had been preserved as pure breeds since ancient times. Cleveland Bays were called "Chapman horses" because they carried traveling salesmen ("chapmen").

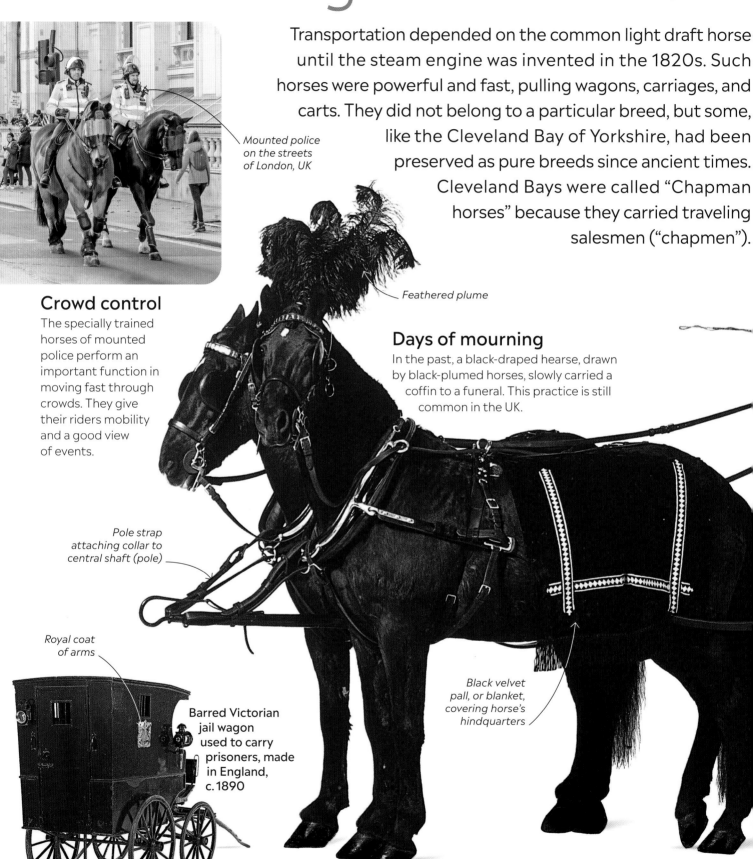

Mounted police on the streets of London, UK

Crowd control

The specially trained horses of mounted police perform an important function in moving fast through crowds. They give their riders mobility and a good view of events.

Feathered plume

Days of mourning

In the past, a black-draped hearse, drawn by black-plumed horses, slowly carried a coffin to a funeral. This practice is still common in the UK.

Pole strap attaching collar to central shaft (pole)

Royal coat of arms

Barred Victorian jail wagon used to carry prisoners, made in England, c.1890

Black velvet pall, or blanket, covering horse's hindquarters

Sunday morning drive

This 19th-century print of a family outing in a horse-drawn carriage is by American lithographers Nathaniel Currier and James Ives.

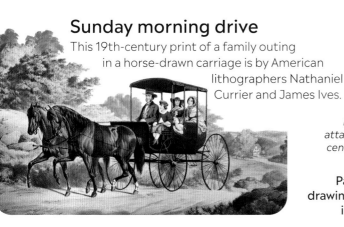

Harness attached to center pole

Pair of horses drawing a phaeton in Turin, Italy

Regency man about town

In European spa towns in the early 19th century, young gentlemen dashed about in elegant sporting phaetons, driven with the top up or down.

Driver dressed in dark mourning suit

Plumes made of ostrich feathers

Coffin

Engraved glass sides

Splinter bar to which traces are attached

Pair of black Welsh Cobs, in black and silver harness, pulling funeral hearse, made in England, c.1850

Rubber-wheeled dairy wagon, made in England, c.1950

R. JORDAN & SONS

THE PADDOCK

North American horses

Indigenous wild horses of North America became extinct 10,000 years ago. Domestic horses, from whom the mustang descended, arrived with Christopher Columbus in 1492 and became symbols of freedom and enterprise. Horses have been faithful companions, pulling heavy loads in desert heat, down dark mines, and along muddy roads. The horse gave some Indigenous peoples their fastest transport.

Buffalo Bill

In 1882 rider Buffalo Bill Cody (1846–1917) held the first professional rodeo show at the Fourth of July festivities in Nebraska.

Travel today

The Amish settled in Pennsylvania in the 1700s, developing the Conestoga (a heavier version of the covered wagon) to explore the West. Their simple lifestyle sees them still using horses for work and travel.

A musical ride

The Royal Canadian Mounted Police are famous for their pageantry, wearing red tunics, and riding black horses in a musical ride.

Stetson hat

Stock whip

Saddle horn

Fringed leather jacket

Flowing mane

Western curb bit

Leather chaps, or trousers

Leather stirrups

The Appaloosa with its distinctive spotted coat is a favorite mount of the Niimíipu (Nez Perce) people.

Cowgirl in typical Western clothes riding 14-year-old skewbald cob

Legendary ladies

Calamity Jane, Annie Oakley, Belle Starr... the list of legendary women of the Old West is endless, when cowgirls shot guns and rode horses. Bad guys like Frank and Jesse James, and Billy the Kid were chased by lawmen like Wyatt Earp and Wild Bill Hickok and everyone rode a horse.

Buffalo hunt

American artist George Catlin painted the Indigenous peoples on horses hunting buffalo, which all but disappeared in the West due to slaughter by European colonizers.

Army roughriders

Ordinary cavalrymen (an army's mounted forces) spent hours in the saddle, so strong horses were essential. American artist Frederic Remington painted the US Cavalry in hot pursuit.

All in the family

Cattle ranchers have been part of the lore of America's West for a long time. Movie cowboys and their horses, such as the Lone Ranger and Silver, recreated the legend of the Old West. Currently, there are over 700,000 cattle farms and ranches in the US. Mostly family owned, 58 percent of the ranches have been in the same family for at least three generations.

Lasso for roping cattle

Stetson

Saddle horn

Silver and tooled leather gunbelt

Western curb bit

Cowboy riding a palomino

Sporting horses

Legend goes that Pelops drove a four-horse chariot to found the Olympic Games in 1222 BCE.

Four-horse chariot races were part of the early Olympic Games, while centuries later, the Romans raced horses in special arenas. In the 11th century, flat racing first began in England, before riding schools teaching classical equitation started in Europe. In 1750, the Jockey Club was founded in England. Today, competitive sports with horses are as popular as ever.

Every year in Siena, Italy, horses and riders race around the main square in the exciting *Palio*.

Throatlash

Over they go
To jump over obstacles in their path is part of the natural behavior of wild horses that are galloping away from a predator. Domesticated horses will also jump when directed to do so by their riders. To train a horse to be a show jumper is a long and complicated process.

Point to point
Amateur steeplechasing began in 1752 as a cross-country race. A church steeple was the goal, and all the hedges or gates had to be jumped to reach it.

In cold water
Three-day eventing tests the endurance, speed, and obedience of a horse, as well as its rider's ability. The event is broken down into dressage on the first day, followed by a cross-country course with a water hazard (right), and show jumping on the third and final day.

Adolfo Cambiaso

Cambiaso is a world-renowned polo player from Argentina and a noted breeder of polo ponies. Regarded as the best polo player in the world, Cambiaso has been riding since he was two years old. He has been interested in horse breeding since childhood and currently has around 1,000 horses.

Fun for everyone

Mounted games, or gymkhanas, offer young riders a chance to see what they and their ponies can do at this junior level of equestrian, or horse riding, competition.

Riding sidesaddle began with European royalty about 600 years ago.

Rein

Hard hat

Classic jodhpurs, or riding pants

Anyone for polo?

Polo was invented by the Chinese about 2,500 years ago. Today, it is popular in Argentina, the US, Australia, and the UK. Two teams of four players each hit the ball with longhandled mallets and try to score as many goals as possible. The team with the most goals wins.

They're off!

Modern flat racing—racing on a track with no obstacles—owes its existence to the Thoroughbred, first developed in England in the 17th and 18th centuries.

Horseplay

The close bond, forged over thousands of years, between humans and horses cannot be broken by the rise of the automobile. The horse is popular in competitive sports, and those who cannot take part in these can watch on TV or attend the events in person. Horses must be carefully trained to maintain their fitness and optimize their chance of winning. Racehorses use their natural instincts to run as part of a herd. Show jumpers and dressage horses mix training with obedience. Horses provide sport and recreation, from pony-trekking and endurance racing to international driving and classical equitation.

Away at the races

Flat racing—the "Sport of Kings"—is popular around the world with classic races such as England's Derby, America's Belmont Stakes, and Australia's Melbourne Cup.

Racers taking part in the Tattersalls Irish Guineas Festival at The Curragh Racecourse in Kildare.

Creek crossing

Pony-trekking is a popular recreation for both adults and children. Here, some children are riding ponies across a shallow section of the Gannel River in Newquay, Cornwall, UK.

Hunters return

Around 2500 BCE, Assyrians on horseback hunted lions or wild oxen. Later, in Europe, as in this 16th-century Flemish calendar, the quarry was the stag, bear, or hare. By the 17th century, the English developed fox-hunting, helped by trained scent hounds. Today, fox hunting with hounds is banned in most of the UK.

HORSE WALK

The horse has four gaits, or natural ways, in which it moves. These are walk, trot, canter, and gallop. Horses can also be taught to move in certain specialized ways.

Walk has four beats—left hind, left fore, right hind, and right fore legs.

Canter has three beats—left hind, left fore and right hind together, and finally right fore leg.

Trot has two beats—left hind and right fore together, right hind and left fore together.

Gallop has four beats, but the footfall pattern is different from the walk. All feet come off the ground.

Elegant dressage

Classical riding, or dressage, shows the horse at the peak of its fitness and its obedience to its rider. It peaked in popularity during the 18th century. In modern advanced dressage competitions, marks out of ten are given for excellence.

Horses cannot wear boots in dressage

Driving test

At horse shows, driving events are popular. In 1970, the first international horse-driving trials took place. These trials had presentation and dressage on the first day, followed by a marathon of 9 miles (15 km), and then obstacle driving on the third day.

Pacers and trotters

In North America, France, Russia, Wales, and Australia, the trotting, or harness, race is as popular as flat racing. The modern trotting race is similar to ancient chariot races, except that it is a single trotting horse. In pacing, legs move in lateral (same side) pairs.

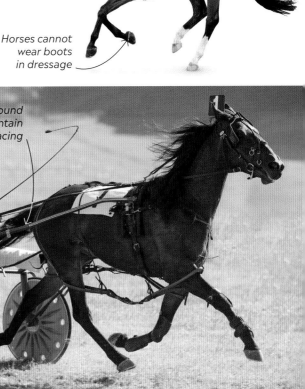

Special harness around legs helps horse maintain its lateral pacing

Useful **ponies**

Children who learn to ride and look after a pony acquire an understanding of the rich relationships that can exist between humans and animals. In the past, the native ponies of northern Europe were used as pack animals and farm workers. When a docile pony was too old to work, it was given to a child for riding lessons. At that time, almost everyone could handle a horse. Today, very few people learn to ride or have a pony, but for those who do, it is a very rewarding experience.

Through all kinds of weather
Pony Express riders experienced bad weather, tough terrain, and conflict with Indigenous peoples to carry the mail 2,000 miles (3,300 km) across the US in the 1860s.

Pair of black Shetland ponies hitched to a cart loaded with hay and a bag of feed

Small but mighty
Shetland ponies were bred as farm animals and, despite their size, they can draw heavy carts.

Riding for all
Anyone who wants to ride should have the chance to do so. A gentle ride on a pony can boost well-being and confidence, and it provides outdoor exercise.

How to look after your pony
To be responsible for a pony is hard work, as the animal's welfare is dependent on its owner. The pony must have pasture, fresh water, shelter, exercise, and companionship. It must be groomed and inspected for parasites.

Straw for bedding

Rolled oats can be fed to competition horses, for extra energy

Sugar beet (must be soaked for 12 or 24 hours before feeding)

Rolled barley

Blue-glazed toy showing a boy and his pony, found in Egypt, c. 200 CE

Various types of rugs or sheets may be used in certain situations to keep the pony warm, or protect it from flies in hot weather.

Dressage whip

Lunge whip

Headcollar to catch and lead the horse

Around and around

Every fairground has a merry-go-round, or carousel, on which children can safely ride a brightly painted mechanical horse.

Hoof pick

Moulting brush

Plastic curry comb for removing dried mud

Soft body brush

Metal comb used when plaiting

Hay for eating

Miner's lamp

Pit ponies

Ponies were often taken to work down coal mines as they could carry heavy weights. It was wet, cold, and dark, with many miners and ponies living underground for months on end.

A young boy and his blue roan Shetland pony ready for working underground in a coal mine

Three-tined fork for mucking out stables

63

Did you know?

AMAZING FACTS

The head of this herd of horses is probably a mare.

A herd of horses is usually led by a mare (a female horse). She decides when the herd should move on to look for fresh grazing. The mare leading the herd uses behavior like the bite threat to keep the herd in order.

A horse drinks at least 44 pints (25 liters) of water daily—about 13 times more than a person.

"Horsepower" is an internationally recognized unit of the pulling power of an engine. Scientists define it as the power that is required to lift a weight of 165 lb (75 kg) over a distance of 39 in (1 m) in 1 second. A real horse is 10 to 13 times as strong as this.

People argued for years about whether a horse takes all four feet off the ground when it gallops. In 1872 photographer Eadweard Muybridge set up a line of 24 cameras and photographed a horse galloping past. The pictures proved a horse has all four feet off the ground.

Donkey carrying a load of straw

"Doing the donkey work" means doing hard, boring work. The expression comes from the fact that donkeys were bred for their stamina and endurance to carry heavy loads.

A mare and her foal

Within an hour of being born, a foal can stand and walk. A child takes about a year to master the same skills. This ability is essential for the foal to move on with the herd.

Horses have powerful lungs and strong hearts to help them run fast. A Thoroughbred's heart can weigh 11 lb (5 kg), which is 16 times heavier than an adult person's heart.

The Shire horse is the largest breed of horse, but the biggest horse ever was a Percheron called Dr. LeGear. He measured 84 in (21 hands/213 cm) high.

The expression "straight from the horse's mouth" means to hear something directly from the best source. It comes from the best way to discover the age of a horse, which is to examine its teeth. As a horse ages, its incisor teeth wear down and protrude much more.

20-year-old horse shows its teeth

QUESTIONS AND ANSWERS

Why do newborn foals look so gangly?

When a foal is born, its legs are already 90 percent of their adult length, whereas the rest of its body has to grow a lot. This makes it look gangly. Foals often bend their front legs to reach down to eat grass.

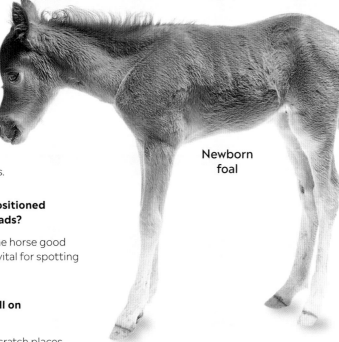

Newborn foal

Why are horses' eyes positioned on the sides of their heads?

This eye position gives the horse good all-round vision, which is vital for spotting potential dangers.

Why do horses often roll on the ground?

Rolling helps a horse to scratch places it can't otherwise reach and to shed loose hairs from its coat. Each horse leaves its individual scent on the rolling patch. These scents mix together to produce a unique "herd smell" that helps the herd to bond.

How did the Przewalski's horse get its unusual name?

The Przewalski's horse is named after the man who discovered it—Nikolay Przhevalsky. This 19th-century Russian explorer traveled around eastern central Asia. His wildlife discoveries included the wild camel and wild horse, which he found in western Mongolia in the 1870s.

RECORD BREAKERS

 Highest jump
The world record for the highest horse jump is 8 ft 1.25 in (2.47 m) by Captain Alberto Larraguibel Morales from Chile riding Huaso in 1949.

 Speed record
The fastest winner of the Epsom Derby in England was a horse called Workforce, who completed the 1.5-mile (2.4-km) course in just 2 minutes 31.33 seconds in 2010.

 Biggest breed
The largest breed of horse is the Shire horse, which stands 68–76 in (17–19 hands/173–193 cm) high.

Smallest breed
The smallest breed of horse is the Falabella, which is just 30 in (7.2 hands/76 cm) high.

How fast can a horse run?

The maximum recorded speed for a galloping horse is 43 mph (69 kph). This puts the horse among the 10 fastest mammals in the world, but way behind the fastest animal, the cheetah, which tops 65 mph (105 kph).

A horse rolling

Why do horses run away?

Horses facing danger have two options— fight or flight. They nearly always run away. One horse is always on guard. If it senses danger, it alerts the others and all of the herd runs off.

When was horse racing first invented?

The first records of a ridden race come from the ancient Greek Olympic Games in 624 BCE. It took place over about 1,313 yds (1,200 m).

Why do horses come in so many different shapes and sizes?

People have created different types of horse by selective breeding. This means breeding is limited to selected animals, by cross-breeding between horse types or in-breeding within a family. This can produce a specific skill, such as strength or speed. Distinctive breeds have emerged over time.

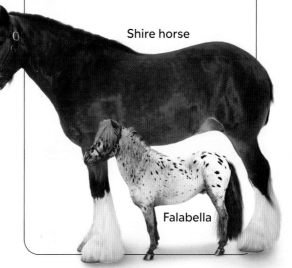

Shire horse

Falabella

Identifying breeds

There are about 400 different breeds and types of horse around the world. Many were developed for specific purposes.

PONIES

11

American Shetland
This pony, from the Shetland Islands, was taken to the US in 1885.

Each horse's typical height is given in hands (1 hh = 4 in/10 cm), next to the hand symbol.

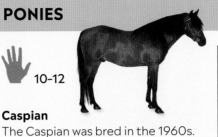

10-12

Caspian
The Caspian was bred in the 1960s. It is an ancestor of the Arab horse.

12.2-14.2

Connemara
Fast, courageous, and good at jumping, this Irish pony is ideal for competitions.

up to 15

Haflinger
The Austrian Haflinger pony is always chestnut or palomino in color with a distinctive flaxen mane and tail.

13-14

Fjord pony
This Norwegian pony is used for riding, carrying loads, and pulling plows. Its mane is usually cut short.

Under 12

Welsh mountain pony
Thanks to its origins in the Welsh mountains, this hardy pony is able to survive on minimal rations.

RIDING HORSES

14 and over

Appaloosa
This horse has a distinctive spotted coat. It is descended from horses brought to the Americas by the Spanish conquistadors.

14.1-15.1

Arab
The Arab is the purest breed of horse. It comes from the Arabian peninsula, where it was in existence as early as 2500 BCE.

13.3-15

Barb
This breed comes from Morocco, where it was the mount of the Imazighen. It is normally gray or black in color.

14.3-16

Quarter horse
This was the first American breed of horse. It was used for farm work and herding cattle and made a perfect cattle rancher's horse.

15.1 and over

Selle Français
This horse's name means "French saddle horse." It was bred for riding, and today is used for showjumping as well as racing.

16-17

Thoroughbred
This is the fastest and most valuable of all the breeds of horse. The Thoroughbred is used primarily for racing.

DRIVING HORSES

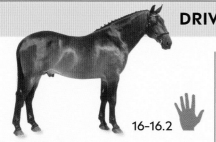

16–16.2

Cleveland Bay
Bred in the northeast of England, the Cleveland Bay was used to carry hunters and to pull carriages.

15.2 and over

Friesian
This horse from the Netherlands was often used to pull funeral carriages because of its black color.

15.2–16

Gelderlander
Bred specifically to pull carriages, this Dutch horse is often used in carriage-driving competitions.

12.2–14

Hackney
The British Hackney has a high-stepping gait. It was bred to pull carriages, especially the famous Hackney Cab.

14.2–15.2

Lipizzaner
The white Lipizzaner horse is used at the Spanish Riding School in Vienna, where it excels at displays of dressage.

14.2–16

Standardbred
This American horse is the world's best breed for harness racing. It can cover 1 mile (1.6 km) in under two minutes.

DRAFT HORSES

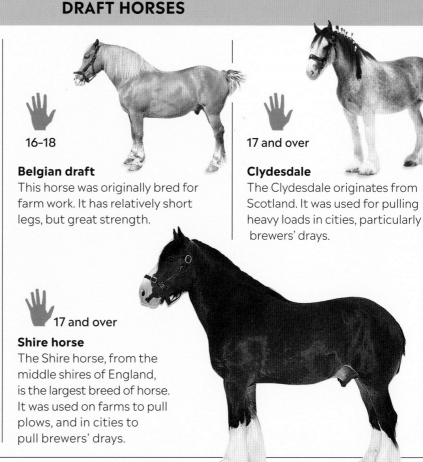

15–16

Ardennais
Originating from the Ardennes region of France and Belgium, this is the oldest of the European heavy breeds.

16–18

Belgian draft
This horse was originally bred for farm work. It has relatively short legs, but great strength.

17 and over

Clydesdale
The Clydesdale originates from Scotland. It was used for pulling heavy loads in cities, particularly brewers' drays.

15–19

Percheron
The French Percheron has been used for pulling coaches, farm work, and riding.

17 and over

Shire horse
The Shire horse, from the middle shires of England, is the largest breed of horse. It was used on farms to pull plows, and in cities to pull brewers' drays.

Find out more

If you would like to get more involved in the world of horses, there are lots of ways to do it. You could visit a horse show or a county 4-H show where many breeds of horses are often on display. Why not try going riding? Once you have learned the basics, you can go pony-trekking in the countryside, or even enter a local competition yourself.

Ribbons
Ribbons and rosettes are given to the winners in riding competitions. Usually red signifies first place, blue second, yellow third, and green fourth. Tricolor rosettes are given for championships.

Tricolor rosette

Going riding
The US Hunter Jumper Association lists recognized riding academies on its website, to help you find a school in your area. The school may provide you with a hard hat, but it is a good idea to wear long pants and a long-sleeved top to protect your skin if you fall off.

Visiting a horse show
You can see horses in sports such as showjumping, dressage, and driving events at horse shows. They range from a riding club's gymkhana or point to point racing, to county and international shows.

You must wear a hard hat at all times when riding.

Ear bonnets help to protect a horse from flies and cut out distracting sounds.

Knocking down this pole would incur four faults.

Equipment
After two or three lessons, if you decide you want to continue riding, you could invest in some riding clothes. The first and most important things to buy are riding boots, a hard hat, and some riding gloves.

Jodhpurs are more comfortable for riding than ordinary trousers.

USEFUL WEBSITES

- **US Equestrian Federation** (usef.org/about-us): The national governing body. Its website includes info about rules, breeds, education, and safety.
- **American Horse Council** (horsecouncil.org): Advocates for the equine industry. Website includes a directory of related businesses.
- **US Hunter Jumper Association** (www.ushja.org): Unifies and represents the hunter and jumper disciplines through education, recognition, and programs.

Pony Club silver trophy

All Camargue horses are the same gray color. Younger animals may be darker, but their coats lighten with age.

Camargue horses socializing

Seeing horses in the wild

Wild horses still roam in protected Herd Management Areas in 10 western US states. Several breeds of ponies live wild in the UK. Most ponies are owned by local breeders, but getting too close will frighten them. Further afield, herds of wild Camargue horses live in France.

Shire horses pulling a plow

Seeing different breeds of horses

Your local county fair is a good place to see horses. Many breeds are at 4-H events in individual states. Abroad, you can see Andalusian horses at Jerez in Spain, and Lipizzaners at the Spanish Riding School in Vienna, Austria.

PLACES TO VISIT

HORSE EVENTS AND SHOWS

- **Kentucky Derby:** The most prestigious horse race in the United States. This high-stakes race features Thoroughbred horses. It takes place each year the first Saturday of May in Louisville, Kentucky.

- **Land Rover Kentucky Three-Day Event**: The first and longest-running annual five-star eventing competition in North America. It showcases the highest level of equestrian eventing and welcomes people from all over the world.

- **All-American Quarter Horse Congress:** The world's largest single-breed horse show. Its mission is to protect and promote the Quarter Horse and support owners, breeders, exhibitors, and enthusiasts. It is held every year at the Ohio Expo Center in Columbus.

- **Hampton Classic Horse Show:** One of the largest outdoor horse shows in the US in Bridgehampton, NY. About 1,400 horses participate in the Classic every year in more than 200 different competitions.

- **Devon Horse Show**: The oldest and largest outdoor multi-breed horse competition in the US, held in Devon, Pennsylvania.

ACTIVITIES

- **International Museum of the Horse,** located in Kentucky, is dedicated to exploring the history of all horses and their impact on human civilization and is a resource for horse researchers around the world.

- **Wild Horse Museum**, located in Corolla, NC, is open year-round and provides information on the Spanish mustangs that run wild in the Currituck Outer Banks.

A racehorse being exercised

Glossary

ARAB One of the oldest breeds of horse. Arab horses originated in the Arabian peninsula, where they were bred by the Bedouin people about 3,000 years ago.

ASS A member of the horse family. There are three types of asses—African wild ass (*Equus africanus*), and Asian wild asses (*Equus hemionus* and *Equus kiang*).

BARB One of the earliest horse breeds. The Barb comes from North Africa, and is the mount of the Imazighen.

BIT The part of a bridle that fits in the horse's mouth. Different styles of bit include the snaffle, curb, and pelham.

BLAZE A white marking on a horse's head.

BRIDLE The headgear used to control a horse.

BRUMBY A type of feral horse found in Australia.

CADANETTE One of the long cords formed when the coat of a Poitou donkey is not groomed regularly.

CANTER A gait in which the horse's feet hit the ground in three beats.

CENTAUR Mythical creature from Greek mythology, half-man and half-horse.

CHIVALRY The qualities expected of a knight in the Middle Ages, such as courage, honor, and courtesy.

African wild ass

Bridle

COLDBLOODS The name given to an ancient group of horses from northern Europe. Modern-day heavy or draft horses, such as the Shire horse, Percheron, and Jutland, are descended from these horses.

COLT A male horse that is less than four years old.

CROSS-BRED An animal produced by breeding between two horse family members, or between two horse breeds.

DOMESTICATION Donkeys were domesticated in western Asia and Egypt about 7,000 years ago, followed by horse domestication in what is now present-day Russia.

DONKEY A domesticated ass, descended from the African wild ass (*Equus africanus*).

DRAFT HORSE A horse used to pull heavy loads and work the land, rather than for riding.

DRESSAGE A competition in which a rider shows a horse's skills in obedience.

EQUIDS Members of the horse family of mammals, which includes domestic horses, wild asses, and zebras.

EQUITATION The art of horse-riding.

FERAL An animal that is descended from domesticated ancestors, but has returned to live in the wild.

FETLOCK Part of a horse's leg that sticks out just above and behind the hoof. A tuft of hair often grows at the fetlock.

FILLY A female horse under four years old.

FLAT RACING Racing horses on a track with no jumps or other obstacles.

FORELOCK The tuft of hair on a horse's forehead.

GALLOP A fast gait in which the horse's feet hit the ground in a four-beat gait, and then all four feet briefly come off the ground.

GAUCHO A cattle rancher from the South American pampas. Gauchos use horses to round up their cattle.

HAND A unit of measurement used to work out a horse's height. One hand is 4 in (10.16 cm). A horse's height is measured from the ground to the top of its shoulders, called the "withers."

HARNESS The equipment of straps and fittings used to fasten a horse to a cart or other vehicle.

HINNY An animal produced by interbreeding a horse and a donkey. A hinny has a horse father and a donkey mother.

Dressage

Mane

HOOF The horny part of a horse's foot.

HORSEPOWER A unit of power used to measure an engine's pulling power. One horsepower is the power required to lift a weight of 165 lb (75 kg) a distance of 39 in (1 m) in one second and is equal to 746 watts.

HOTBLOODS The Thoroughbred and eastern breeds of horse, such as the Arab and Barb. The name comes from the hot countries of North Africa and Arabia in which these breeds originated.

JENNY A female donkey.

JOUST A combat between two mounted knights in the Middle Ages to practice fighting skills.

LIGAMENT A band of fibrous tissue that links two bones and allows a joint to move freely.

MANE The long hair that grows from the back of a horse's neck.

Przewalski's horses

MARE A female horse aged four or more.

MULE An animal produced by breeding between a horse and a donkey. A mule has a donkey father and horse mother.

MUSTANG A feral horse in North America.

MUZZLE A horse's nose and mouth area.

ONAGER Another name for the Asian wild ass (*Equus hemionus*).

PACE A two-beat gait in which two legs on the same side of the horse move forwards.

PACK ANIMAL An animal used to carry loads.

PIEBALD A horse's coat with large, irregular patches of black and white.

POINTS External parts of a horse, such as its poll, pastern, withers, and fetlock.

PONY A horse not over 58 in (14.2 hands/147 cm) high.

PRZEWALSKI'S HORSE The sole surviving wild horse, found only in zoos and reserved parks at present. This horse became extinct in Mongolia in the 1960s, but is being reintroduced from herds bred in captivity.

RODEO A competition in which North American cattle ranchers show off their skills at horseriding and handling cattle.

SHOWJUMPING A sport in which horses are ridden around a course, featuring fences to jump.

SIDESADDLE A position in which both the rider's legs are on the left side of the saddle.

SKEWBALD A horse coat, with large white patches on any coat color other than black.

SPUR A U-shaped device fitted to a rider's boot heels, used to urge a horse forward.

South American spur

STALLION A male horse who is four or more years old, and has not been castrated.

STEEPLECHASE A race over fences and open ditches.

STIRRUPS Two leather loops suspended from either side of a horse's saddle with metal footrests to support the rider's feet.

STRIPE A long, white stripe on a horse's head.

THOROUGHBRED A horse whose ancestry can be traced back to one of three famous stallions.

Thoroughbred

TROT A two-beat gait as diagonal pairs of feet hit the ground at the same time.

WALK A four-time gait in which each of the horse's legs hits the ground separately.

WARMBLOODS Breeds of horse that are crosses between hotbloods and coldbloods.

WITHERS The top of a horse's shoulders.

ZEBRA A member of the horse family, found in Africa, that has a coat patterned with black and white stripes.

Index

Acknowledgments

Dorling Kindersley wish to thank:
Alan Hills, Dave Gowers, Christi Graham, Sandra Marshall, Nick Nicholls, and Barbara Winters of the British Museum, and Colin Keates of the Natural History Museum for additional special photography; Clubb Chipperfield Limited, Foxhill Stables & Carriage Repository, Suzanne Gill, Wanda Lee Jones of the Welshpool Andalusian Stud, Marwell Zoological Park, the National Shire Horse Centre, Harry Perkins, and the Whitbread Hop Farm for lending animals and vehicles for photography; The Household Cavalry for providing the rider and the drum horse, and The Knights of Arkley for the jousting sequence; The Berrriewood Stud Farm, Carol Johnson, and Plough Studios for their help in providing arenas and studios for photography; Dr Alan Gentry of the Natural History Museum, Christopher Gravett of the Royal Armouries (HM Tower of London), and Rowena Loverance of the British Museum for their research help; Kim Bryan for editorial consultancy; Céline Carez, Hannah Conduct, Liz Sephton, Christian Sévigny, Helena Spiteri and Cheryl Telfer for editorial and design assistance; David Ekholm-JAlbum, Sunita Gahir, Susan Reuben, Susan St Louis, Lisa Stock, and Bulent Yusuf for the clipart; Neville Graham, Sue Nicholson, and Susan St Louis for the wallchart; Andrea Mills for text editing; Deepak Negi and Manpreet Kaur for picture research assistance; Helen Peters for the index; Ann Baggaley for proofreading; Raven Kame'enui-Becker for a North American authenticity review.

The publisher would like to thank the following for their kind permission to reproduce their images:

Picture credits:
t=top, b=bottom, c=centre, l=left, r=right
Alamy Stock Photo: Jules Annan 58br, Art Collection 3 34–35t, Arterra Picture Library 24cr, 41bc, BIOSPHOTO 25clb, © chrisstockphotography 6tr, Cultura Creative RF 2tr, Gainew Gallery 42bc, Galopin 39tr, Steven Goodier 6–7bc, GRANGER – Historical Picture Archive 55tl, The Granger Collection 46cb, Grant Heilman Photography 14bl, Heritage Image Partnership Ltd 42–43c, The History Collection 39cla, horsemen 41cra, 52cl, imageBROKER. com GmbH & Co. KG 36cl, Images of Africa Photobank 18clb, INTERFOTO 31cr, Juniors Bildarchiv GmbH 36cra, Ton Koene 24cb, Library Book Collection 9br, Minden Pictures 21tc, Hilary Morgan 59clb, Keith Morris 61b, Nature Picture Library 21cra, 37tr, Christopher Nicholson 20clb, North Wind Picture Archives 35cra, 63clb, Luc Novovitch 46cl, Sam Oaksey 31b, Paul Terry Photo 59tc, PhotoStock-Israel 18–19b, Pictorial Press Ltd 47cc, Pictures Now 44tl, Daniela Porcelli / SPP-JP / SPP Sport Press Photo 61crb, Kseniya Ragozina 34cla, Paul Rollins 13tr, Sally Anderson News 62bl, Gordon Scammell 60clb, Skyscan Photolibrary 21tl, Anna Stevenson 15bc, Sergey Uryadnikov 36–37b, Renato Valterza 55tr, Mike Walker / Gillian Higgins at www.horsesinsideout.com 10bl, Liam White 50tr, Jennifer Wright 27tl, YA / BOT 57tl, YG-Tavel-Photos 24–25b. **American Museum of Natural History:** 8cl, 9br. **Ann Ronan Picture Library:** 6tr. **Barnaby's Picture Library:** 43tr. **Bob Langrish:** 41br, 66–67. **Bridgeman Images:** Peter Newark American Pictures 35br, 62tr, With special authorisation of the city of Bayeux 31tc, 41tl Archiv fur Kunst & Geschichte, Berlin; 24tr British Library; 49tl Guildhall Library; 39cb Harrogate Museums and Art Galleries; 35t, 41tl, 56tl, 59cr Private Collection; 32bl Musée Condée, Chantilly. **Dorling Kindersley:** 37cl Dave King (by courtesy of the National Motor Museum, Beaulieu); 27tr, 36tl, 38 (all except 38br), 40bl, 41 (all except 41tl, 41crt, 41br), 50c, 51tl, 51tr, 51c, 51cl, 56bl, 63bc Bob Langrish; James Mann, courtesy of Harvey Stanley 37cla, Bob Langrish / Lady Fisher / Pegasus, Kilverstone Wildlife Park 65br. **Dreamstime.com:** Lynn Bystrom 19ca, Vladimir Cheberkus 12c, Gorshkov13 16cb, 17cra, Iliyan Kirkov 59tc (white horse), Sergii Kumer 68–69bc, M. Rohana 58cla, Magryt 63tr, Cristina Villar Martin 10tc, 64br, Darlene Munro 56cl, Lefteris Papaulakis 21br, Pfluegler 15tr. **Getty Images:** Fine Art Images / Heritage Images 23bl, Matt Browne / Sportsfile 60–61c, Photographs by Maria itina / Moment 14–15c, Seb Daly / Sportsfile

59br, imageBROKER / David & Micha Sheldon 15cr, Scoop Dyga / Icon Sport 61c, Troy Harrison / Moment 12–13b, Robbie Jack / Corbis Entertainment 43cla, Fredrik Lerneryd / AFP 19cr, Leon Neal / Staff 40crb, Dan Tuffs 57clb, Feng Wei Photography / Moment Open 17crb, Westend61 58–59c. **Getty Images / iStock:** cmannphoto 58clb, Thepalmer / E+ 4bl. **Hirmer:** 33tl. **Hulton Picture Collection:** 53br. **Jim Lockwood, Courage Shire Horse Centre, Berks:** 67bl. **Kentucky Horse Park, U.S.A** 67cb. **Mary Evans Picture Library:** 32tr. **The Metropolitan Museum of Art:** Gift of Several Gentlemen, 1911 57bl. **Michael Holford:** 31tc, 47tc. **Mike Dent:** 23tl. **National Museum Of The American Indian, Smithsonian Institution:** 10 / 9628 34clb. **naturepl.com:** Kristel Richard 13cr, 37c. **Oxford Scientific Films:** 17tc/Anup Shah/Okapia. **Pegas of Kilverstone, Lady Fisher, Kilverstone Wildlife Park, Norfolk.** **Peter Munt, Ascot Driving Stables, Berks:** 67tr. **Peter Newark's Western Americana:** 55tl, 62t. **Prince D'elle, Haras National De Saint Lo, France:** 66bc. **Robert Harding Picture Library:** 21cr, 24cb, 48cr, 56cr. **© Royal Armouries:** 2crb, 42tc, 45tc, 45cra. **Samantha A. Brooks:** Matti Moyer, UF / IFAS 25cra. **Shutterstock.com:** Ed Goodacre 52br, Leonid Maximenko 15cb, David Muscroft 47b, Abdul_Shakoor 54tl. **Spin way Bright Morning, Miss S. Hodgkins, Spinway Stud, Oxon:** 66tr. **SuperStock:** 3LH-Fine Art 34bc. **SWNS:** 46bc. **The Board of Trustees of Royal Armouries:** 2c, 42tr, 45tc, 45cr. **Trustees of the British Museum:** 4ctr, 7br, 16tl, 17bl, 22tl, 22cl, 22br, 23tr, 26tr, 28c, 33tr, 33bl, 46br. **Whitbread Brewery:** 13cr.
Illustrations: John Woodcock

Wallchart:
The Trustees of the British Museum: tl.
Alamy Stock Photo: Paul Rollins cra

All other images © Dorling Kindersley

For further information see:
www.dkimages.com